TURKEY

No security without human rights

AI Index: EUR/44/84/96
ISBN: 0 86210 263 4

First published in October 1996 by
Amnesty International Publications
1 Easton Street
London WC1X 8DJ
United Kingdom

Original language: English

Printed by: Alden Press, Oxford

CONTENTS

Glossary

ANAP	Motherland Party
CHP	Republican People's Party
DEP	Democratic Party
DHKP-C	Revolutionary People's Liberation Party-Front
ECPT	European Committee for the Prevention of Torture
EU	European Union
HADEP	People's Democratic Party
HEP	People's Labour Party
HRA	Turkish Human Rights Association
IBDA-C	Islamic Raiders of the Big East-Front
ICCPR	International Covenant on Civil and Political Rights.
MGK	National Security Council
MIT	Turkish intelligence agency
MLKP	Marxist-Leninist Communist Party
NATO	North Atlantic Treaty Organization
OSCE	Organization for Security and Co-operation in Europe
PKK	Kurdish Workers' Party
SBP	Socialist Unity Party
SHP	Social Democratic Populist Party
TBKP	Turkish United Communist Party
TIHV	Turkish Human Rights Foundation
TIKKO	Turkish Liberation Army of Peasants and Workers
TMA	Turkish Medical Association
TKP	Turkish Communist Party
TÜMTIS	Turkish Union of Motor Vehicle Workers
UK	United Kingdom
UN	United Nations
UNHCR	(Office of the) United Nations High Commissioner for Refugees
USA	United States of America

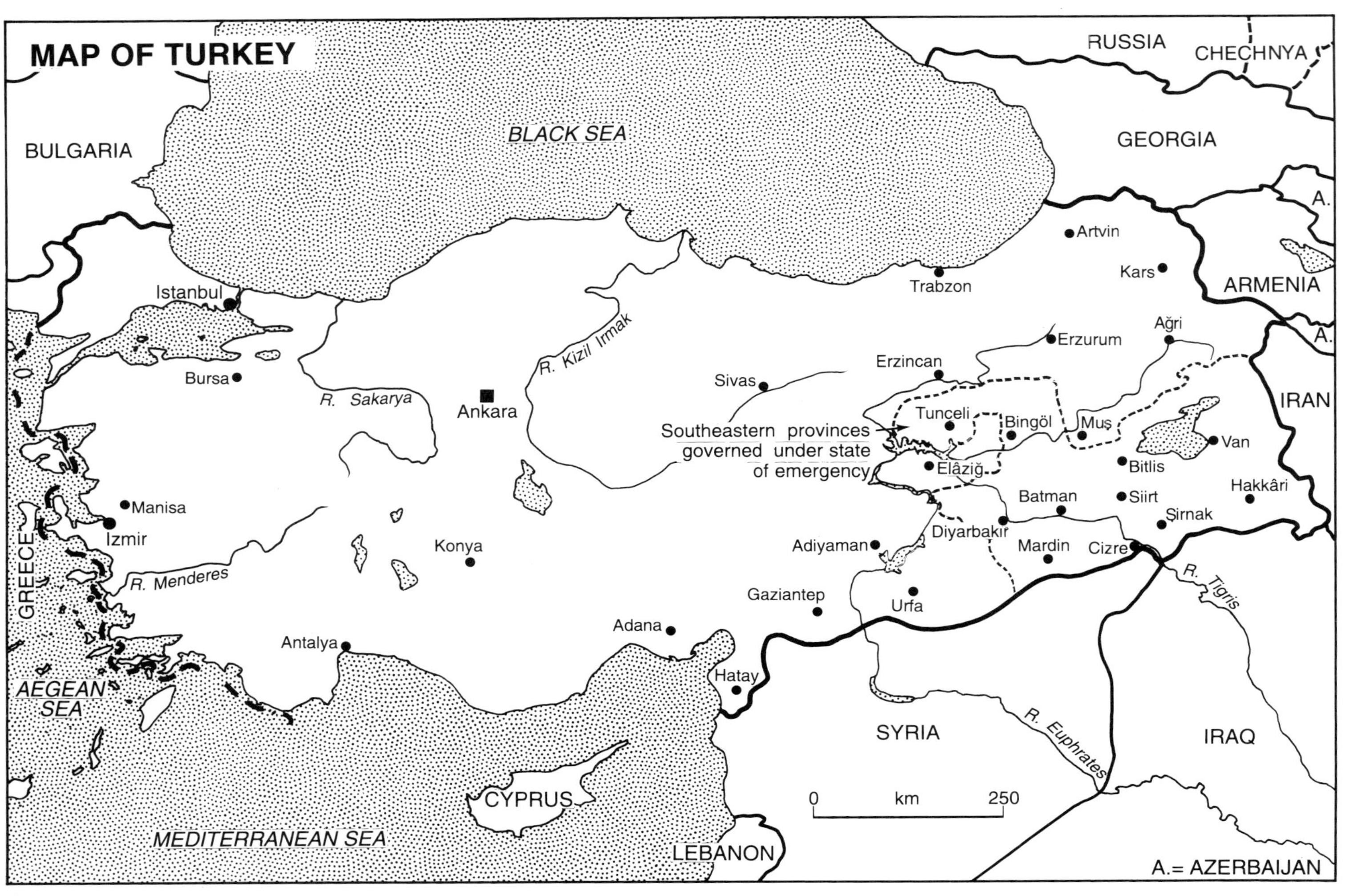
MAP OF TURKEY
RUSSIA
CHECHNYA
GEORGIA
BULGARIA
BLACK SEA
A.
Artvin
Kars
ARMENIA
Trabzon
Istanbul
A.
Ağri
Erzurum
Erzincan
R. Kizil Irmak
Bursa
Sivas
IRAN
R. Sakarya
Ankara
Tunceli
Bingöl
Muş
Van
Southeastern provinces
governed under state
of emergency
Elâziğ
Bitlis
Hakkâri
Manisa
Batman
Siirt
Şirnak
Izmir
Diyarbakir
Konya
Adiyaman
Mardin
Cizre
R. Tigris
R. Menderes
Gaziantep
Urfa
GREECE
Adana
Antalya
Hatay
AEGEAN
SEA
SYRIA
R. Euphrates
IRAQ
CYPRUS
0
km
250
MEDITERRANEAN SEA
LEBANON
A.= AZERBAIJAN

INTRODUCTION

"We'll finish terrorism but we are being held back by democracy and human rights."

Turkish Deputy Chief of Staff,
General Ahmet Çörekçi, July 1995[1]

Recent Turkish history has been dominated by the Turkish state's failed experiment in maintaining security through repression. Successive governments have made some progress towards establishing parliamentary democracy and fundamental freedoms, but national security — internal as well as external — has consistently been left to the discretion of the security forces. They have treated international human rights standards and Turkish law with equal disdain.

As a result, the human rights picture in Turkey is bleak. Torture or ill-treatment have long been routinely inflicted on people detained for common criminal offences as well as on political charges. "Disappearance" and extrajudicial execution are new patterns of violation which appeared in the early 1990s and have since claimed hundreds of lives. Turkish citizens do not enjoy true freedom of expression. During the past six years scores of prisoners of conscience have served terms of imprisonment for expressing their non-violent opinions. Hundreds more, including writers and artists, are being tried in State Security Courts and threatened with imprisonment because they dared to express their political views.

This report is based on information collected from a wide range of sources including testimony given by victims and their families, statements given by witnesses and lawyers, medical reports and legal documents, photographic and videotape evidence, information given in replies by the Turkish Government, public documents issued by intergovernmental organizations, newspaper reports and reports issued by non-governmental organizations. The report includes the findings of 10 investigative research missions to

Turkey and numerous trial observations carried out by Amnesty International since 1990. It proposes a modest set of reforms which, if supported by real political will, could radically improve human rights in Turkey.

A state of insecurity

Since 1960 elected government in Turkey has lived in the shadow of the unelected state within the state: the interior and defence ministries, regional governors and, most importantly, the military, the police force and the intelligence agencies. In the past 36 years the military have overturned three governments, suspended three parliaments and closed legally established political parties.[2] Under the Constitution drawn up by the military junta in 1982 the security forces continue to exert a powerful influence over the government through their membership of the National Security Council (MGK).

Martial law courts have hanged a prime minister and two other ministers, tried members of parliament and imprisoned thousands of civilians, some of whom have been in jail since the 1980s. Army officers still prosecute and judge civilians in State Security Courts.

Life is already insecure for Turkish people. Turkey is situated in a politically unstable region and has experienced two decades of intense political violence by armed opposition groups, principally the Kurdish Workers' Party (PKK), which have attacked and killed civilians. The state has responded with a wide range of "security" measures which, by violating basic human rights, have further endangered the personal security of individual citizens. Despite all the promises of reform, Turkish citizens can still be swept off the streets and into a police station or gendarmerie post, where they may be held for up to a month. There they will be unprotected by even the most basic safeguards against torture, still a standard method of interrogation. Since 1980 more than 400 people have died in police custody, apparently as a result of torture.

The exact status of security forces allegedly responsible for violations is sometimes hard to establish, particularly in the southeast, where security forces do not always wear standard uniform or insignia. In most reports of torture, the detainee was interrogated by plainclothes police officers of the Criminal Investigation or Anti-Terror branches or by gendarmes.

Gendarmes are soldiers who carry out police duties in rural Turkey. Many allegations of extrajudicial execution have been made against members of Special Operations Teams. These are technically police officers under the authority of the Interior Ministry, heavily armed for close combat with the PKK. Special Operations Team members frequently accompany members of the paramilitary village guard force and gendarmes in security raids on villages. Regular army and air forces also participate in large operations in the southeast.

While the Turkish Government has talked publicly of progress on human rights, the situation has in fact gone from bad to worse. In the early 1990s, as the existing "tough measures" proved insufficient to overcome political violence, police and gendarmes turned to criminal methods. This has resulted in more than 100 "disappearances" and an unprecedented wave of extrajudicial executions that has claimed hundreds of lives.

The Turkish Government routinely denies, covers up or justifies torture, extrajudicial executions and "disappearances" by its security forces. The record shows that ministers will say anything rather than squarely confront the gendarmerie and police commanders with the evidence of their abuses. In 1994, faced with irrefutable reports that soldiers were burning villages in Tunceli province, the Interior Minister first suggested the villagers were torching their own homes and then that the PKK were destroying villages while dressed as gendarmes.

"Even if I saw with my own eyes that the state had burned a village, I would not believe it"[3], said the then Prime Minister Tansu Çiller when she was told by a delegation of village leaders that soldiers supported by helicopters had destroyed their villages. As security "embarrassments" must always be justified by referring to Turkey's internal and external enemies, she suggested that the helicopters could belong to the PKK (which does not have an air force), Russia, Afghanistan or Armenia.

Internal and external threats, real or imagined, are used to legitimize human rights violations by the security forces. Without supervision by parliament and government, safeguards against human rights violations have inevitably and consistently been ignored.

Modern Turkey is plagued by a number of political anomalies, the legacy of years of military rule, which appear to be wholly at odds with the general direction in which the country

HASAN OCAK
GÖZALTINDA

is developing. While Turkey has one of the most sophisticated newspaper and publishing industries in the world, and recently launched its own communications satellite, television producers and musicians are tried in military courts, academics and novelists are imprisoned, and newspapers are closed because they have dared to question the actions of the state.

The Turkish Government asserts that it prosecutes and punishes members of the security forces who torture or unlawfully kill. Publicly available sources suggest that there are few such prosecutions and even fewer convictions. Under its international treaty obligations the Turkish Government is required to take effective steps to prevent human rights violations, as well as prosecute the perpetrators and compensate the victims. The fact that authorities have not taken even the most basic steps necessary to comply with treaty obligations suggests that there is a deliberate policy of acquiescence to widespread and gross human rights violations at the highest level. That successive governments have ignored recommendations and standards which have been in place for decades further illustrates the lack of commitment to human rights by those at the top.

State of emergency

The persistence of political violence since the late 1960s is a serious factor that cannot be ignored. The two armed opposition groups most active since the 1980 coup are the PKK, who have a large force in the mountains of the east and surrounding countries, and the Revolutionary People's Liberation Party-Front (DHKP-C), formerly *Devrimci Sol,* who have attacked police and military targets in the cities of the west. Both groups proclaim an ideology of liberation but are also known for killing non-combatant civilians and prisoners. PKK forces have frequently killed Kurdish villagers taking no part in the conflict, as well as civil servants. Teachers have been a particular target; 90 have been killed by the PKK since 1984.

The conflict between security forces and the PKK in south-east Turkey, where most of the estimated 12 million Kurds live, has unquestionably contributed to the deterioration in respect for human rights throughout the country. The PKK began attacks

---

Left: ***Emine Ocak protests against the "disappearance" of her son, Hasan Ocak. Since the early 1990s more than 100 people have "disappeared" in Turkey. © Ş. Dayanan***

in August 1984 with the goal of establishing a separate Marxist Kurdish state. The organization now professes more limited aims — principally a degree of autonomy for the southeast.

A state of emergency in force in the 10 provinces most affected by the conflict gives the security forces wide-ranging powers. The State of Emergency Region Governor controls the armed and police services in the region and can assume control of any functions of the civil administration. The governor and the forces at his disposal also enjoy a high degree of official immunity from prosecution.

Some generals and police chiefs argue that respecting human rights will obstruct their efforts to combat armed opposition groups. Even if this were true, it would be no excuse for condoning torture or "disappearance", but the last 16 years of brutal and repressive methods which have unambiguously failed to

Two men detained by the security forces during an operation against the PKK in southeast Turkey. © Popperfoto

deliver public security make a poor argument for yet more brutality and repression. Others have admitted that the strategy of trying to achieve security through repression has not only failed but is actually compounding the problem. Retired general Nevzat Bolugiray suggests in his memoirs: "While the people's trust in the state may have been eroded as a result of persecution committed by the authorities with their state mentality, there may have been drifting towards the PKK at the grassroots level."[4]

The former Human Rights Minister, Algan Hacaloğlu, made a similar observation: "The PKK is still recruiting people. Why? Because there is widespread alienation, because despite talk [the government] have not been able to apply real progress for rights, democracy."[5]

All citizens are placed at risk when the forces of the state step outside the law. Even the state's own agents can become victims.

On 15 December 1995 the PKK unilaterally declared a ceasefire. Four weeks later the authorities announced that the PKK had massacred a group of 11 men, seven of them village guards, in a minibus which was then set on fire. The Chief of General Staff flew journalists from all the major newspapers and broadcasting organizations to Güçlükonak, Siirt province, the remote scene of the massacre. The then Prime Minister, Tansu Çiller, commented: "These enemies of humanity who disbelieve that the state authority has weakened and turned their guns on our innocent citizens will definitely drown in the pit they have fallen into. Such attacks against the existence of the Turkish Republic prove how just we are in the struggle against terrorism."

Shortly afterwards, doubts about the official story began to emerge, chiefly from the families of the victims. A delegation drawn from a wide spectrum of international, professional and human rights organizations investigated the massacre and gathered evidence which indicated that those responsible were actually government forces.

Time for change

Much of Turkish civil society clearly thinks that it is time to set a new agenda. Prominent figures in public life, the arts, media and industry have expressed their shame that people continue to be jailed for voicing non-violent dissident opinions. When Süleyman Demirel, now President of Turkey, issued election campaign advertisements in 1991 promising a new openness — "the walls of police stations will be made of glass" — the public responded positively. That promise was never fulfilled, but the people are still waiting.

Public expressions of anger and fear at persistent human rights violations reached a new level following a series of outrages committed in the name of security during 1995 and early 1996. In March 1995, 23 people were shot dead on the streets of Istanbul by plainclothes police officers who opened fire on a turbulent protest against police inaction over an armed attack on a café. "Disappearances" in Istanbul following these disturbances led to widespread alarm. In January 1996 Metin Göktepe, a photographer covering the funeral of political prisoners, was detained by police officers and later found beaten to death. In the same month a member of parliament uncovered evidence that a group of youngsters, one as young as 14, had been severely tortured at Manisa Police Headquarters in west Turkey.

There was strong public reaction to these incidents because ordinary people recognized that the victims of these violations could have been their own sons or daughters. These incidents did not take place in the mountains of the southeast, but on the streets of the nation's largest city and in a provincial town near the Mediterranean coast. Without proper safeguards and accountability, extraordinary "security" measures put everyone at risk.

If some important elements of Turkish society are clearly calling for reform, the international community is inconsistent in its response. Governments who have most influence on the Turkish Government — members of the North Atlantic Treaty Organization (NATO) and particularly the governments of the European Union (EU) — are holding back from using the tools they themselves have developed to combat human rights violations through the Council of Europe, the Organization for Security and Co-operation in Europe (OSCE) and the United Nations (UN). When challenged on their inaction, these governments echo the Turkish Government's excuse: their hands are tied by the threat of terrorism. The real reason for their reluctance to take a strong stand is no mystery. Turkey is a valued ally

Right: ***Special Operations Team member on guard in Diyarbakır. The security forces cannot provide true security for Turkish citizens unless they respect human rights. © R. Maro***

and is seen as a strategic bulwark against instability in parts of the Middle East and the countries of the former Soviet Union. Turkey is also an important trading partner, and a lucrative market for military equipment.

Real security needs human rights

This report shows that the notion that national security can only be effectively protected at the expense of respect for human rights is fundamentally flawed. Under international law, states may take special measures to deal with an emergency which threatens the life of the nation. Although certain rights may be temporarily restricted if strictly necessary and proportionate to the threat posed, basic rights such as the right to freedom from torture and the right to life may not be suspended under any circumstances. A state of emergency should be an extension of the rule of law not an abrogation of it.

By violating Turkey's own laws with impunity, the security forces are undermining respect for the rule of law in a way that can only serve to fuel the cycle of violence and perpetuate abuses. Without respect for human rights there is no prospect of security for Turkey's citizens.

The reforms necessary to bring Turkey into line with, for example, the European Convention for the Protection of Human Rights and Fundamental Freedoms (European Convention on Human Rights), which Turkey ratified in 1954, are neither complex nor expensive. They are no more than an extension of principles already recognized in Turkish law, reinforced by political will.

1

Silencing dissent

The question of freedom of expression in modern Turkey reflects a grim paradox. Since the late 1980s the number of prisoners of conscience known to Amnesty International has fallen from hundreds to about a dozen in January 1996. At the same time, freedom of expression is under an assault unprecedented since the 1980 military coup. The risk of imprisonment for the written word may be lower for a Turkish journalist or human rights defender of the 1990s, but the risk of being killed is very much higher.

Turkish civil society can be proud of the considerable progress it has made in re-establishing freedom of expression since military rule ended in 1984. Under the generals, all political parties and most trade unions were banned, and hundreds of people were tortured and imprisoned for their peaceful beliefs. Most prisoners of conscience had been prosecuted under the notorious Articles 141, 142 and 163 of the Turkish Penal Code, which imposed long terms of imprisonment for advocacy of communism, Kurdish "separatism", or religion-based government. Many people were imprisoned for belonging to organizations which had operated openly and legally before the military coup.

For the first four years after the military coup, even moderate opinion was gagged. Newspapers were regularly censored or confiscated and their journalists prosecuted. It was during this period that the military attempted the complete suppression of the Kurdish language. Law 2932, passed in 1983, punished with imprisonment anyone who conveyed any idea in "languages which are not official languages of other nations". Political prisoners who delivered their defence speeches in Kurdish received additional prison sentences.

Throughout the 1980s some political parties, trade unions and other organizations campaigned against these laws and numerous others which restricted political freedom and punished dissent, arguing that they were unnecessary and inappropriate constraints in a modern society.

A step towards freedom of expression

The military junta of 1980, which ruled in the last decade of the Cold War between East and West, had tried to legitimize itself as a bulwark against communism. By 1990, six years after Turkey returned to parliamentary rule, the opinion that a healthy society needs free and open political debate was being strongly argued by sections of the media and by many members of parliament. Left-wing groups which did not advocate violence were no longer perceived as such a profound threat and there were fewer prosecutions of their members. Trials of members of Islamist political organizations under Article 163 had more or less stopped. The Turkish Communist Party (TKP), outlawed since the 1920s, began to operate openly as the TBKP and later as the Socialist Unity Party (SBP).

These gains in the right to freedom of expression were won by many politicians, writers and activists who risked torture and imprisonment to challenge censorship. The then Prime Minister, Turgut Özal, reflected the changing mood when he announced that there should be "a talking Turkey".

In April 1991 Articles 141, 142 and 163 of the penal code were repealed and the relatively small number of prisoners of conscience were released. Law 2923 was repealed at the same time and this was soon followed by the publication of Kurdish language newspapers, books and many collections of Kurdish poetry, although education and broadcasting in Kurdish remained illegal.

The Motherland Party (ANAP) broke the government monopoly on broadcasting in the early 1990s. There are now hundreds of independent radio stations and scores of local and satellite television stations. Political and social issues are being discussed in the broadcast media, newspapers and magazines with an openness unimaginable a decade before. Turkish citizens have more access to information and ideas than ever before. Public scandals are uncovered and condemned by the news media, who have grasped the new freedom to challenge and criticize the government of the day in the most outspoken terms.

Set against this picture of a society engaged in lively and

open debate is a collection of severe restrictions to freedom of expression which continue to be imposed on those issues which the state considers vital to its integrity: maintaining the dignity of the army and the security forces, the institution of military service and, above all, defeating Kurdish "separatism". The state controls comment and reporting on these issues through legal and illegal means. Imprisonment is the principal method of legal control.

In 1954 Turkey became a party to the European Convention on Human Rights, Article 10 of which guarantees the right to freedom of expression. Nevertheless, despite reforms Turkey's laws and practice continue to violate the country's treaty obligations and its own Constitution.

The reforms of the Turkish Penal Code in April 1991 were made as part of the Anti-Terror Law (Law 3713). Activities contained within that law's widely drawn definition of "terrorism" include non-violent forms of political dissent. Article 142 ("disseminating propaganda undermining national pride") was replaced with the similar offence of "separatist propaganda" under Article 8 of the Anti-Terror Law.

Article 8 — targets of prosecution

The Anti-Terror Law, in Article 8, punished any expression of separatism, whether violent or not, with long terms of imprisonment and heavy fines. Initially, there were few prosecutions, cases moved slowly and often resulted in acquittal, with the result that in 1992 there were very few prisoners of conscience. In July 1993, in response to an intensification of the conflict in the southeast, the prime minister and the chief of staff called for media support in a "total war" against separatism. Thereafter, although Article 28 of the Turkish Constitution states: "The Press is free, and shall not be censored", journalists and others who openly opposed government policy in the southeast ran the risk of prosecution and imprisonment.

The second half of 1993 and the first months of 1994 saw a dramatic increase in detentions and prosecutions under Article 8. Those imprisoned included lawyers, political activists, trade unionists, academics, writers, publishers and journalists.

Ayşe Nur Zarakolu, director of the *Belge* (Document) publishing house, served a five-month sentence in 1994 under

Expressions of Kurdish "separatism" are punished severely, even if they are not committed on Turkish soil. In 1994 Mehdi Zana was sentenced to a term of imprisonment under Article 8 of the Anti-Terror Law for speaking on human rights in south-east Turkey at a press conference at the European Parliament in Brussels.

Article 8 of the Anti-Terror Law for publishing *The Republican People's Party Program (1931) and the Kurdish Problem*, by Ismail Beşikçi, an author currently imprisoned under Article 8. *Belge*, established in 1977, has published numerous political books and, by giving a platform to Armenian, Greek and Kurdish authors, has challenged a number of Turkey's contemporary political taboos. As a result, Ayşe Nur Zarakolu has been repeatedly prosecuted by the authorities and has been imprisoned three times. She has been involved in various political, publishing and trade union activities, and is a member of the Istanbul branch of the Turkish Human Rights Association (HRA).

Persecution for "separatist propaganda" extended to academics. Fikret Başkaya, assistant professor at the Faculty of Economics at Abant University in Bolu, was arrested on 17 March 1994 to serve a 20-month sentence under Article 8 for his book, *Westernization, Modernization, Development — Bankruptcy of the Paradigm*, an examination of the socio-economic evolution of Turkey since the 1920s. One chapter of his book deals with Turkey's Kurdish minority, which he described as a discrete ethnic group. He served his sentence at Haymana Prison, on the outskirts of Ankara.

Thought-crime does not even have to be committed on Turkish soil to be punished under the Anti-Terror Law. On 13 May 1994 Mehdi Zana, the former mayor of Diyarbakır, began serving a two-year prison sentence under Article 8 for a press conference in Brussels in which he read out the testimony he had just given before the Human Rights Sub-Committee of the European Parliament.

A prominent figure in the Kurdish community, Mehdi Zana has always pursued a conciliatory approach to the Kurdish question. In the early 1980s his steadfastly non-violent political activities earned him prison sentences amounting to 31 years from a military tribunal. He was released in May 1991 as a result of a partial amnesty under the Anti-Terror Law, which provided for a conditional reduction of all sentences by varying percentages. He spent the early 1980s under the horrific regime of Diyarbakır Military Prison, where he was severely tortured for long periods. In his testimony to the European Parliament, for which his latest sentence was imposed, he said:

> *"Like all Kurds sentenced for the 'crime of separatism', I have been stripped of my political rights for life ... I should perhaps make it clear that while I continue to campaign peacefully for the recognition of the rights of the 15 million Kurds living in Turkey, I am not a member of any party or movement."*

Leyla Zana, Mehdi Zana's wife, is one of four Kurdish former members of parliament who had their parliamentary immunity lifted in March 1994 and were prosecuted by Ankara State Security Court. Winner of the Sakharov Prize for Freedom of Thought, Leyla Zana is currently in Ankara Closed Prison serving a 15-year sentence. She was convicted of membership of an illegal organization after an unfair trial in a state security court.

Mehdi Zana was released in December 1995 but faces eight more years in prison if outstanding sentences against him are upheld on appeal.

The authorities justify their use of Article 8 on the grounds that Turkey has a grave security problem. However, those imprisoned under the special provisions of Article 8 have employed no weapon more violent than a pen or a microphone. In fact, several prisoners have strongly criticized armed opposition movements — at personal risk of reprisal in some cases. Lawyer Ahmet Zeki Okçuoğlu, who served a 20-month sentence under Article 8 for participating in a round-table discussion on the problems of the southeast, gave an interview to the daily newspaper *Cumhuriyet* (Republic) just before commencing his sentence on 13 January 1994:

> *"For years I have clearly declared my opposition to terrorism and opposed violence. In my whole life I have never used a weapon. I have opposed those who have taken up arms. But the state has tried me as a terrorist and convicted me. Now I am branded as a terrorist throughout the world."*

The growing number of prosecutions under Article 8 provoked increasing disquiet, not only in the mainstream media, but also among leading politicians and even members of the government. Former Culture Minister Fikri Sağlar went so far as to visit Fikret Başkaya and Haluk Gerger, former Secretary General of the Turkish UN Association, both imprisoned under Article 8. He told them: "I feel the dishonour of this shame and ask your forgiveness. After a time, society will ask your forgiveness. We are trying to put an end to this disgrace".[6]

The debate on whether or not to amend Article 8 has proceeded with complete disregard for the fact that it violates international law and standards. In July 1994 Amnesty International submitted the cases of three prisoners convicted under Article 8 to the UN Working Group on Arbitrary Detention. In May 1995 the Working Group declared the imprisonment of the three men to be "a violation of their right to freedom of opinion and expression". The Working Group requested Turkey to take the necessary steps to remedy the situation by bringing Article 8 into conformity with the Universal Declaration of Human Rights and the International Covenant on Civil and Political Rights (ICCPR).

Meanwhile, Turkey's foreign relations were beginning to affect the issue. Turkey was in the process of concluding a customs union with the EU. The terms had been agreed with the EU Commission but had to be approved by the European Parliament. Members of the European Parliament, mindful of Turkey's steadily worsening human rights record in general, and particularly the case of Mehdi Zana who was imprisoned after addressing them at their own invitation, were reluctant to approve the agreement without some progress on human rights.

The Turkish general elections were approaching. The Islamist *Refah* (Welfare) Party, which was expected to perform well, was questioning Turkey's links with Europe. EU governments were eager to see the customs union approved in order to strengthen the pro-European faction in Turkey's political community. It became clear that the European Parliament would approve the customs union in exchange for no more than a gesture towards human rights reform. A gesture was all the Turkish Government would offer.

'Reform' of Article 8

In late October 1995 President Demirel approved amendments to Article 8 under which "separatist propaganda" remains an imprisonable offence, even when the defendant has in no way advocated violence, but the phrase "irrespective of the methods and aims and ideas" was removed. Maximum sentences were reduced from five to three years, and courts were given discretion to impose fines or suspended sentences for first offences. Most of those imprisoned under Article 8 were released pending retrial.

The government claim that the new version of Article 8 represents a real change is contradicted by developments since October 1995. When sentences were reviewed under the new wording of the law most released prisoners' sentences were confirmed, although their original sentences were usually reduced by half or suspended. These prisoners remain at liberty until their sentences are confirmed on appeal. On 10 November 1995 Ankara State Security Court retried Mehdi Zana for his speech at the European Parliament in Brussels and sentenced him to two years' imprisonment under the new version of Article 8.

Several people convicted under Article 8 remained in prison despite the changes. The former member of parliament and President of the Party for Democracy and Renewal, Ibrahim Aksoy, imprisoned in Ankara Central Closed Prison since October 1995 for various writings, was not released. On 23 November 1995 Konya State Security Court retried him for a speech he gave at a political meeting in 1991 and, in the light of the new wording of Article 8, changed its previous sentence of 20 months' imprisonment to 10 months. Amnesty International considered him a prisoner of conscience.

The blind lawyer Eşber Yağmurdereli may be imprisoned

until 2018 because of a speech he gave referring to Turkey's Kurdish minority in Istanbul on Human Rights Day 1991. On 15 December 1995 Istanbul State Security Court sentenced him to 10 months' imprisonment under the revised form of Article 8. If he loses his appeal he will serve this sentence and the remainder of a suspended life sentence for a different offence, imposed by a military court after an unfair trial in the 1980s.

In 1995 Turkey's most renowned living writer, the novelist Yaşar Kemal, was tried under Article 8 by Istanbul State Security Court for an article he had written for the German magazine *Der Spiegel* (*The Mirror*). He was acquitted. In protest at his prosecution, 1,080 intellectuals, writers, publishers and artists put their names to a book titled *Freedom of Thought in Turkey*, a collection of articles by people imprisoned or on trial for their writings. The government responded by charging 185 members of the group under Article 8. Those charged represent a major section of Turkey's literary and artistic elite. Their trials are continuing; the latest was opened in February 1996. On 7 March 1996 Yaşar Kemal was given a 20-month suspended sentence for an essay titled "Dark Cloud over Turkey", his contribution to *Freedom of Thought in Turkey*. The conviction was for "inciting

Yaşar Kemal (left) and his publisher Erdal Öz in court in Istanbul in March 1996. Turkey's best known writer was given a 20-month suspended jail sentence for an article condemning government policy in the southeast. © AP

hatred" under Article 312, which has been used increasingly by prosecutors since the change to Article 8.

In public discussion of freedom of expression in Turkey, much attention has been given to Article 8. In fact, prisoners of conscience are held under several other laws and articles of the Turkish Penal Code which punish criticism of revered public figures and institutions with heavy terms of imprisonment. Those who write about the Kurdish minority are not the only people regarded as enemies of the state and imprisoned in Turkey.

On 14 February 1995 Ankara Criminal Court sentenced Mahmut Kaçar to four and a half years' imprisonment for "insulting the founder of the Republic" under the Law to Protect Atatürk (Law 5816). Mahmut Kaçar, a post office worker, had been detained in Ankara in November 1994 when he interrupted the annual memorial ceremony for Kemal Atatürk, the founder of the Turkish Republic. Mahmut Kaçar had approached the president and ministers holding up a copy of the Koran and

Criticism of state institutions carries severe punishments under the Turkish Penal Code. In February 1995 Mahmut Kaçar was sentenced to four and a half years' imprisonment for "insulting the founder of the Republic" under the Law to Protect Atatürk. © Anadolu Ajansi

saying: "I call you to the Koran ... Turn to God". He described his motives as follows: "My only guide was the Koran. I wanted to communicate the truth to people effectively through a live broadcast ... I have tried to do what a Muslim should. People can choose for themselves." Mahmut Kaçar's speech contained no advocacy of violence and Amnesty International considers him a prisoner of conscience. The sentence was upheld by the Appeal Court on 17 April 1995.

Freedom of association under attack

In 1995 constitutional reform greatly eased the restrictions on freedom of association contained in the 1982 Constitution imposed by the generals, and formalized in the military government's Law on Trade Unions, the Law on Political Parties and the Law on Associations.

Outside the militarized areas of the southeast the state tolerates most political debate in controlled environments such as newspaper columns or on television panels. Politics on the streets is another matter. Law 2911 on Assembly and Demonstrations puts many restrictions on demonstrations and posters. They have to be authorized by local governors, who frequently prohibit them. Although the law provides for prison sentences of up to three years, Turkish citizens who wish to demonstrate publicly often resort to what they describe as "pirate" demonstrations, risking arrest and beatings. When asked by a television reporter why he had beaten an elderly woman demonstrating against the activities of Russian security forces in Chechnya on 31 January 1995, a police officer replied that it had been a mistake — he thought she was a left-wing protester.

The law as well as brute force was used to suppress a campaign by families of victims of "disappearance". On 1 June 1995 the HRA began a campaign against "disappearance". Under Law 2911, the governors of both Istanbul and Ankara refused permission to use a wall poster for the campaign showing a picture of a pair of shoes and the words: "An end to 'disappearances' — those responsible must be brought to justice".[7]

On 8 July 1995 police broke up a peaceful sit-down protest

Right: ***Although the freedom to organize is recognized by the Turkish Constitution, in practice trade union activities are often brutally repressed. Bülent Beci, a member of TÜMTIS, was beaten by gendarmes during an industrial dispute in July 1995.***

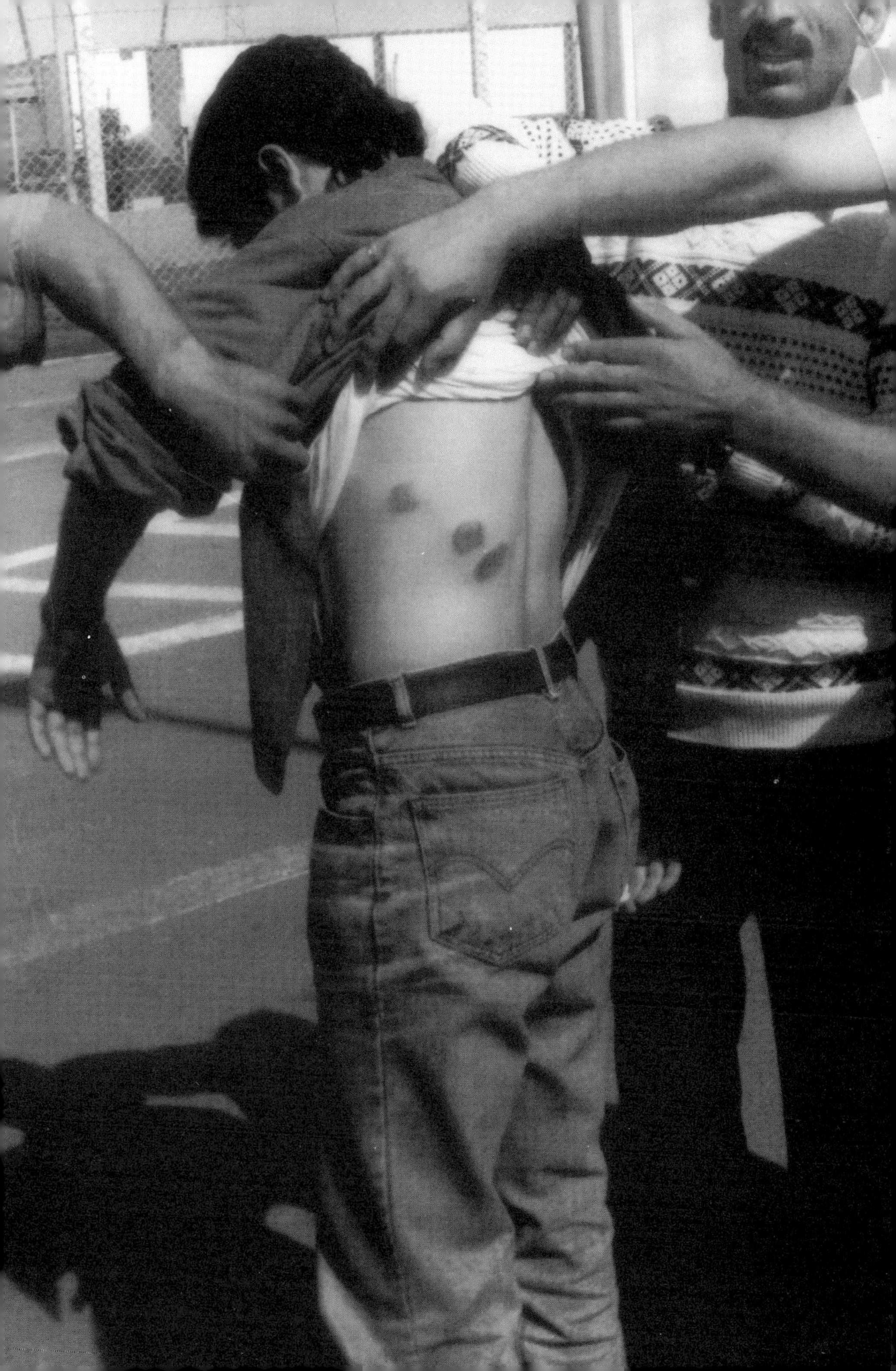

in Istanbul by relatives of the "disappeared". According to the daily newspaper *Cumhuriyet*, 41 people were detained by police wielding truncheons. A lawyer who observed the incident told Amnesty International: "While they were detaining people, they were hitting them. They hit Emine Ocak with a truncheon on the head as they took her into custody — she remained in detention for about 10 hours before being released".

Emine Ocak is the mother of Hasan Ocak, who "disappeared" in police custody in Istanbul in March 1995. His body was later found by police on vacant ground in the Beykoz district and buried as an unidentified person. She was among a group of families who had been demonstrating by sitting down in Istanbul's Istiklal Street every Saturday for the previous month.

On 1 July 1995, 42 people — relatives of Hasan Ocak and others — were detained near his grave in Küçükköy Cemetery and taken to Küçükköy police station where some of the detainees claimed they were beaten, dragged along the ground and tortured while held in custody overnight. Twenty-four of the victims, including Hasan Ocak's sister and mother, made a formal complaint to Gaziosmanpaşa Public Prosecutor and were examined by the Forensic Medicine Institute. The Institute's report has yet to be published. The victims also held a press conference and showed journalists the injuries caused by the ill-treatment. Maside Ocak, sister of Hasan Ocak, told the press conference what happened:

> *"All you could see was truncheons rising and falling, and kicking feet. They put us in police vehicles and drove us to Küçükköy police station where the beating continued. They mainly used truncheons, but they also beat our heads against cupboards. Five of us were taken to Aksaray Anti-Terror Branch, subjected to electric shocks and hanged by the wrists."*

Turkish trade unionists taking industrial action have suffered brutal repression. In December 1995, 43 members of the Turkish Union of Motor Transport Workers (TÜMTIS) were sacked by the transport company Nak-Kargo in Izmir. On 22 December the sacked workers, accompanied by 100 union members and local union leaders, went to Nak-Kargo's headquarters and asked for a meeting with company management. The management refused to see them and riot police broke up the

A human rights worker from the Van branch of the HRA in southeast Turkey takes the testimony of a victim of forced village evacuation. The office has now been forced to close down and the former president of the branch obliged to seek asylum abroad. Human rights defenders have paid a price for their brave defence of human rights; 10 officials of the HRA have been killed in the past five years. © R. Maro

peaceful gathering, beating people about the head with truncheons. Halil Dinç, President of TÜMTIS in Izmir, received a head injury that required seven stitches. When he went to the police station to complain, he told Amnesty International, he was detained for 24 hours, as were the seven trade unionists who had accompanied him. His complaint has not been investigated.

Human rights defenders and advocates under fire

Article 33 of the Turkish Constitution is supposed to guarantee all citizens the right to form associations, but even well-known and respected members of Turkish society have served terms of imprisonment for overstepping the boundaries imposed by the state. In 1991 the state began to resort to the bullet and the bomb in order to deal with its opponents.

The fact that Article 8 of the Anti-Terror Law characterized even non-violent advocacy of separatism as "terrorism" helps to explain official lack of concern at the killing of journalists and political activists. Those who have worked to uncover violations have themselves become targets.

Lawyers are in the frontline of human rights work in Turkey. Eren Keskin, former secretary of the Istanbul brance of the HRA, was provisionally released in November 1995 after serving five months of a sentence imposed under Article 8 of the Anti-Terror Law.

The HRA is an independent organization founded in 1986 to monitor abuses and protect human rights. Since its foundation the HRA has outspokenly condemned violations of human rights. Today the HRA has more than 15,000 members. Many HRA members, however, have paid for their courageous defence of human rights with imprisonment and torture, and sometimes with their lives. No less than 10 HRA members have been killed in the past five years.

There are two principal reasons for the intense pressure on the HRA.

First, the state does not welcome the scrutiny of human rights activists who have helped to document and limit the systematic violation of human rights by interviewing victims, by acting as observers during confrontations between the civilian population and the security forces, by assisting foreign delegations, and by making representations to police, prosecutors and governors. These activities have earned the HRA bitter enemies in the ranks of the government and the security forces.

Second, in the highly charged atmosphere engendered by political violence, opposition to the torture or extrajudicial execution of suspected members of armed opposition groups is often perceived by the authorities as support for those groups. Several HRA officials have been prosecuted for assisting armed organizations, when the real motive for prosecution was apparently the defendant's work against human rights violations.

Lawyers are among Turkey's foremost human rights activists. Eren Keskin, former secretary of the Istanbul branch of the HRA, who was provisionally released in November 1995 after serving five months of a sentence imposed under Article 8, told Amnesty International:

> *"The police see defence lawyers as PKK members ... once, in Istanbul State Security Court, I asked if my client [accused of PKK membership] had any requests. A policeman grabbed me by the waist and wrestled me from side to side several times, dragging me right off my feet. The police are particularly offended by the fact that a female lawyer should take up the case of a PKK defendant. I complained to the prosecutor but he did nothing."*

Article 18 of the UN Basic Principles on the Role of Lawyers states: "Lawyers shall not be identified with their clients or their clients' causes as a result of discharging their functions".

Eren Keskin was one of four lawyers from Istanbul who went to investigate disturbances at Diyarbakır Prison on 3 October 1994 in which dozens of prisoners were seriously injured and two subsequently died. On 6 October the lawyers held a press conference naming a gendarmerie commander and a prosecutor as being primarily responsible. Police stopped two of the lawyers on their way to the airport to leave Diyarbakır and told them, "Do not come again to these parts — we know that you protect these Armenian bastards [meaning Kurds accused of PKK membership]. Do not come again to these parts or we will destroy you." Eren Keskin and another lawyer, travelling separately, were followed to the airport by a white minibus. When they stopped at traffic lights, they were fired on from within the minibus.

Silencing the whistleblowers

The government takes deliberate steps to prevent the violations committed by its security forces being revealed to the Turkish public or the international community.

In November 1993 a group of 14 Diyarbakır lawyers, six of whom had assisted villagers in preparing legal submissions

against Turkey to the Council of Europe's Human Rights Commission, were detained and allegedly tortured during four weeks' incommunicado detention in Diyarbakır Gendarmerie Headquarters.

One of the lawyers detained was Meral Danış Beştaş, secretary of the Diyarbakır branch of the HRA. She reported that during interrogation in Diyarbakır Gendarmerie Headquarters she was slapped, kicked, subjected to sexual insults, stripped of her clothes and hosed with ice-cold water. Tahir Elçi, a lawyer in Cizre, Şirnak province who represented local villagers in numerous formal complaints of human rights violations, said he was tortured and told by police that he would be killed if he continued this work. The lawyers were released pending trials which are still continuing. The indictment includes allegations that several of them had "assisted the PKK" by communicating with human rights organizations within Turkey and in Europe. Although they filed complaints about their treatment, there have been no investigations or prosecutions.

The Turkish authorities also attempt to prevent international scrutiny of their human rights record by banning its foreign critics from entering the country. Foreign journalists and investigative delegations have been removed from the country. Two Amnesty International research delegates have been banned from entering Turkey; one of them was arrested and deported after being held incommunicado for 48 hours. When the *Reuters* news agency began regular detailed coverage of human rights issues, Aliza Marcus, the staff writer responsible, was indicted under Article 312 for "incitement to hatred". She was acquitted, but the Press and Information General Directorate refused to renew her press accreditation. Unable to work, she left Turkey in February 1996.

While foreign journalists and observers can be banned, state agents have used illegal methods to silence local journalists. In the early 1980s journalists were being sentenced to decades in prison. Today, journalists are more likely to be killed because of their work. Turkey has become one of the world's most dangerous countries in which to pursue a career in journalism.

Fourteen journalists covering human rights issues in

Page 26: ***The Istanbul offices of the pro-Kurdish daily* Özgür Ülke *(Free Land) following a huge bomb explosion in December 1994. The attack came after a period of harassment of the publication. © Popperfoto***

DEVRIMCI emek
KATİL DEVLETTEN HESAP SORACAĞIZ
KAHROLSUN TEKELCİ POLİS DEVLETİ
HALKA HÜRRİYET
YIRTACAK

southeast Turkey have been killed, died in custody or "disappeared" at the hands of the security forces since 1992. Most of those killed worked for the Kurdish-owned newspapers *Yeni Ülke*, *Özgür Gündem*, *Özgür Ülke*, and *Yeni Politika*. Each of these newspapers has been forced to close. These newspapers strongly supported Kurdish nationalism, and the security forces clearly considered them "legal organs of the PKK". Eight correspondents and 11 distributors and vendors of these newspapers were murdered in circumstances suggesting state responsibility, and two staff journalists "disappeared". Scores of editors and other staff have been detained and tortured. Many of them are still in prison and on trial or awaiting trial.

Ferhat Tepe, a journalist for *Özgür Gündem*, was abducted in Bitlis in July 1993, reportedly by a man carrying a two-way radio. His father, Ishak Tepe, chairman of the Democratic Party (DEP) in Bitlis, subsequently received telephone calls from a man whose voice reportedly resembled that of a local gendarmerie commander known to be critical of DEP. Ishak Tepe asked the police to investigate the gendarmerie commander's involvement, but was apparently told that they could not interfere. His son's body was later found in a lake 360 kilometres away. The police buried him as an "unknown person", although they had photographs of him and his "disappearance" had received wide publicity. His body was later exhumed and delivered to the family. His father said that there were marks of torture on the body, but a full and independent autopsy was never carried out, a breach of the UN Principles on the Effective Prevention and Investigation of Extra-legal Arbitrary and Summary Executions.

Other family members continued to receive serious threats and suffered police harassment, including repeated detention. In August 1995 Ferhat Tepe's cousin Safyettin Tepe, a journalist on *Yeni Politika*, died in suspicious circumstances in Bitlis Police Headquarters.

In 1992, when a journalist was being killed nearly every month, the Turkish Government reacted with bland compla-

---

Page 28: ***The funeral of journalist Metin Göktepe who was detained by security forces while trying to cover the funeral of prisoners killed at Ümraniye prison in Istanbul and later found beaten to death. Journalists who attempt to monitor the activities of the security forces are at risk in all parts of Turkey.*** **Inset:** ***Metin Göktepe © Ş. Dayanan***

cency. On 11 August Prime Minister Demirel gave his view of the attacks on members of the press: "Those killed were not real journalists. They were militants in the guise of journalists. They kill each other". Such statements reinforced the impression that the murder of those reporting human rights violations in the southeast was not altogether unwelcome to the government.

While there were no official statements condemning the killing of journalists, there were official statements condemning journalists for their writing. A confidential circular from Prime Minister Tansu Çiller to other state departments, dated 30 November 1994, stated:

> *"Activities of certain publications, in particular* Özgür Ülke *... have become clear attacks on the permanent and spiritual values of the state ... With the aim of eliminating such an important threat against the indivisible integrity of the homeland, I ask the Ministry of Justice to determine and pursue the organs that have such publications; to determine why any legally effective processes were not started despite numerous official complaints; to take necessary measures".*

In the early hours of 3 December 1994 the offices of *Özgür Ülke* in Istanbul and Ankara were largely destroyed by high-explosive devices. One employee was killed and 19 others were wounded. The following day the Interior Minister, Nahit Menteşe, suggested that "they may even have bombed themselves". The government statement denying any connection between the circular and the bombing contained a further condemnation of *Özgür Ülke* for "separatism".

While pressure on journalists is greatest in the southeast, reporters covering the activities of the state and its security forces are at risk wherever they work.

Metin Göktepe, a photographer for the daily newspaper *Evrensel* (Universal), was killed on 8 January 1996 while attempting to cover the funeral of prisoners beaten to death on 4 January at Ümraniye prison in Istanbul. Police prevented people assembling to conduct a proper funeral and buried the bodies themselves. Hundreds of people were detained, including Metin Göktepe.

Metin Göktepe's body was found on 8 January at 8.30pm in

the grounds of Eyüp Sports Centre, where the detainees had been taken. A secretly filmed videotape shows detainees in the Sports Centre being ill-treated. An autopsy report issued on 9 January by the Forensic Medicine Department at Istanbul University found that Metin Göktepe had been beaten to death.

There followed several days of official cover-up. The Istanbul Police Chief suggested that Metin Göktepe had fallen and died while trying to escape. Public outrage eventually prompted the Interior Ministry to initiate an investigation. In February the administrative council approved prosecution of 11 police officers for murder. The prosecution was passed to the local administrative council of the Istanbul local governor who blocked prosecution of the Eyüp Police Chief for neglecting his duty and attempting to conceal the death of Metin Göktepe. The trial of the 11 officers continues.

2

'Regret and defiance': torture, 'disappearance' and extrajudicial execution

Systematic human rights violations actually undermine, rather than reinforce, the security of the Turkish state and of the individual Turkish citizen. The "tough measures" which the government has introduced in the name of security violate the human rights not only of alleged members of armed opposition groups but also of vulnerable minorities and ordinary citizens, for whom there can be no security without human rights.

It is important to emphasize that the violations committed by police and gendarmes in the name of the security of the Turkish citizen are criminal offences committed against Turkish citizens. Torture is a long-standing concern, documented by Amnesty International for more than two decades. Failure to eradicate this practice by bringing the perpetrators to justice has led to the proliferation of this and other human rights violations. "Disappearances" and extrajudicial executions have emerged as new and disturbing patterns of human rights violations which have become established in the past five years.

Torture: widespread and systematic

> *"During the first interrogation they grabbed me by the hair and punched my head against the wall. I was thrown to the ground. They kicked me and one officer put his boot into my mouth ... I was spitting blood. They pressed a wooden truncheon against my genitals and twisted it. They laughed, saying: 'She is enjoying this'."*

The victim in this case was Nuray Şen, who was detained on 11 November 1995. After interrogation under torture for 10 days, she was charged with supporting the PKK. She has been released pending her trial and has filed a formal complaint about the torture she suffered.

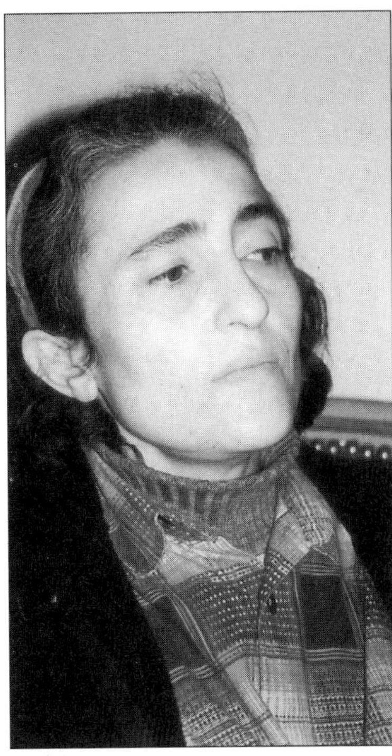

Nuray Şen reported that she was interrogated under torture for 10 days. Her husband had previously been abducted by police officers and later found dead.

It is now a matter of record that torture is widespread and systematic in Turkey, although domestic and international law forbid the torture of any detainee, no matter what the offence. Two intergovernmental organizations, the European Committee for the Prevention of Torture (ECPT) and the UN Committee against Torture, have found that torture is widespread in Turkish police stations, and that Turkish law provides insufficient safeguards against torture.

The ECPT has unique powers to visit member countries and enter places of detention unannounced. In December 1992 the ECPT reported that during an impromptu inspection of Ankara Police Headquarters they had discovered "a low stretcher-type bed equipped with eight straps (four each side), fitting perfectly the description of the item of furniture to which persons had said they were secured when electric shocks were administered to them. No credible explanation could be proffered for the presence of this bed in what was indicated by a sign as being an 'interrogation room'... the delegation's discoveries caused considerable consternation among police officers present; some expressed regret, others defiance". The ECPT also found torture equipment at Diyarbakır Police Headquarters.

In December 1994 the General Director of Security, Mehmet Ağar, (who later became Interior Minister) claimed that people accused of common criminal offences did not complain of torture; allegations of torture, he said, were only made by people interrogated under the Anti-Terror Law with "the aim of undermining the police force's struggle against terrorism".

This is quite simply untrue. No one who finds themselves in police custody in Turkey is safe from torture. Amnesty International has received well-documented allegations of torture and ill-treatment from the very old, the very young, women, members of minority groups, lawyers, doctors, even members of parliament. People have been tortured or ill-treated in connection with common criminal offences, for failing to show their identity cards, or after minor traffic infringements.[8] Haldun Haşmet Aysan, a Ministry of the Interior counsellor who was severely beaten by police in 1992 after being detained for a driving offence in Ankara, was reported by *Hürriyet* (Liberty) as saying: "If this is what happens to people like me, alas for the ordinary citizen."

Sadık Örsoğlu is a member of ANAP, whose leader became

Sadık Örsoğlu, an ordinary Istanbul citizen and long-standing supporter of ANAP, told Amnesty International that he was shocked and angry at being assaulted by police at Yedikule police station when he went to inquire about two detained relatives. He was allegedly beaten and kicked so savagely that he required surgery and had to be fitted with a catheter.

prime minister of Turkey in March 1996. In December 1995 Sadık Örsoğlu went to Yedikule Police Station in Istanbul, to inquire about two relatives who had been detained for alleged involvement in an ordinary criminal offence. He was immediately detained, interrogated and kicked in the genitals so hard that he began to bleed. He was taken to hospital, where he underwent surgery. He was released a week later, but required further surgery and, when interviewed by Amnesty International in March 1996, was still fitted with a catheter. Sadık Örsoğlu expressed considerable anger about the way he was treated by officers of the state: "I will inform the government about what happened to me. And, if the police officer who tortured me is not prosecuted then I will emigrate." The police officer allegedly responsible for torturing him was later suspended and put on trial.

Torture is practised mainly in police stations and gendarmerie posts. It occurs during incommunicado detention before a detainee appears in court. Torture is used to extract confessions, to get information, to intimidate detainees into becoming police informants, and as an informal or summary punishment for petty offences or for suspected sympathy for illegal organizations.

The most common methods of torture are being stripped naked, beating, *falaka* (beating on the soles of the feet), hanging by the arms tied behind the back or bound to a pole, hosing with cold water at high pressure, sexual assault of both men and women, and electric shocks to the mouth, fingers, toes and genitals.

Most of these torture methods were experienced by Ali Ekber Kaya, a civil servant and President of the Tunceli branch of the HRA. He was detained in March 1995 on suspicion of links with the Marxist-Leninist Communist Party (MLKP). In December 1995 he was acquitted of the charge, but he had been severely tortured when he was detained at the Anti-Terror Branch of Tunceli Police Headquarters:

> *"I was taken to the 'torture room'. I had to sit down and they tied my arms to my legs. Then they hosed me with cold pressurized water. They pointed the water jet at particularly sensitive areas of the body such as the kidneys, genitals and rectum. They connected one cable to my foot, the other to my genitals and gave me electric*

shocks... Then they lowered a device from the ceiling. They tied my arms to it and hoisted me up so that my whole weight hung on my arms, then they gave me electric shocks through my fingers and genitals. This went on for three days. Beating and hosing with pressurized cold water continued throughout the first nine days."

Ali Ekber Kaya survived the torture, but two of his ribs were broken. He was released after 11 days in custody. He made a formal complaint about the torture, but there has been no progress in the case. There is no independent and impartial body to investigate such complaints.

Vulnerable people are often among the victims of torture. Hikmet Ercişli, who has learning difficulties, was detained in August 1995 on the outskirts of Kağızman, in Kars province, because he could not produce his identity card when the bus on which he was travelling stopped at a check-point. He was detained by gendarmes, despite protests from the driver and other passengers who had told his family that they would look after him until he reached his sister in Ankara. Hikmet Ercişli remained in custody for two days. The soldiers reportedly stripped him, blindfolded him, beat him and gave him electric shocks. When his relatives went to collect him from the gendarmerie post, the soldiers told them, "We will hand him over if you make no complaint against us". His sister Rahime Ercişli submitted a formal complaint to the local prosecutor but the papers were returned to her. She told the newspaper *Cumhuriyet*:

" I cannot understand how a prosecutor, whose job is to administer justice, can hand back a petition... As a result of being subjected to such inhuman treatment, the psychological state of an already disabled person has broken down still further. To experience such a thing in a democratic country leaves me ashamed of my own humanity."

Particularly at risk of ill-treatment are groups which are viewed with suspicion by members of the security forces, such as the Alawites, a religious minority.

An icy road and a minor accident resulted in a nightmare experience for Sultan and Garip Aygün in January 1995. The couple's car skidded and hit a lamp-post on a bridge in the

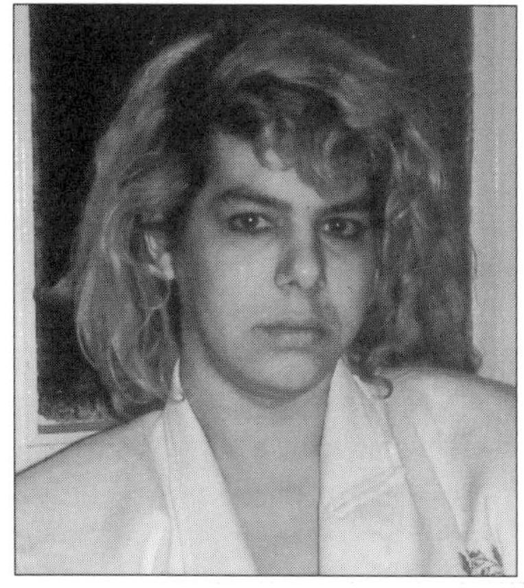

Mustafa Kemal Paşa district of Istanbul. Sultan and Garip Aygün are members of Turkey's Alawite minority and this seems to have been a central factor in what happened subsequently. Later that day they were detained by police officers who asked them to register the accident. At Ümraniye Police Headquarters, the couple were tortured and threatened. Medical reports corroborated their account of their treatment. They complained to the public prosecutor, but by June 1996 no court proceedings had been opened against those responsible. Garip Aygün described their experience:

"We were blindfolded and taken upstairs ... We were accused of having killed a man in the accident and we were asked to sign a statement to that effect. I told them that I was innocent and would not sign such a statement. After that my wife and I were badly beaten. The whole time the officers were cursing and swearing saying that we were Alawites who they would wipe out. They threatened to

---

Groups perceived as having little power have the most to fear when they are taken into police detention. Yaşar Pınarbaş,* (top) *Ilhami Kaya* (middle) *and Seyfettin Turan* (below) *were among 12 transvestites who were reportedly ill-treated at Beyoğlu Police Headquarters in November 1995.

rape my daughters. My wife was called a prostitute. The torture lasted from 4am to 9.30am."

Amnesty International has received many allegations of brutal treatment of transvestites, many of whom live in the Beyoğlu district of Istanbul. In November 1995, 12 transvestites were detained and taken to Beyoğlu Police Headquarters where they were reportedly forced to undress, hosed with ice-cold water and severely beaten. In December 1995 Seyfettin Turan, Yaşar Pınarbaş, Ilhami Kaya, Murat Karafarlı, Ahmet Bozdoğan, Selim Hısar, Ali Bozkuş and Muharrem Kalaycı filed complaints with the Beyoğlu Public Prosecutor. Several of them reported that their hair was pulled out and that they were beaten on their genitals. Medical reports supported their complaints.

Asylum-seekers are another vulnerable group denied proper protection by the Turkish state. Turkey has frequently returned asylum-seekers to situations where they were at risk of human rights violations. Turkey maintains a geographical limitation to the 1951 Convention and 1967 Protocol relating to the Status of Refugees by which non-Europeans (mostly Iranians, Iraqis and Africans) are only granted the right to seek temporary asylum in Turkey until they can be resettled in a third country and their cases are determined by the Office of the UN High Commissioner for Refugees (UNHCR). Asylum-seekers have to register with the local governorship nearest their point of entry within five days and remain there. Amnesty International has received reports of asylum-seekers who have not met the five-day filing requirement being returned to countries where they would face serious human rights violations. Non-European asylum-seekers who have been recognized by the UNHCR but who have not been able to obtain a country of resettlement have also been subject to *refoulement*. Those, on the other hand, who are recognized by the UNHCR as refugees and receive offers of resettlement frequently find themselves stranded. The Turkish authorities deny them exit visas on the grounds that they entered the country irregularly, and in some cases have returned them to their country of origin where they were at risk of grave human rights violations.

Several hundred Africans, displaced from their own countries by political or economic dislocation, live in Istanbul. Some are recognized as refugees by the UNHCR. They are another group who, unprotected by adequate safeguards in law, have learned to expect the worst when taken into police custody.

On 3 March 1995, two Ghanaian citizens (who have asked that their names be withheld) were taken to Beyoğlu Police Headquarters in Istanbul. Both were asked for their passports, which they did not have. One of the detainees produced his police registration letter from the UNHCR which the police officer interrogating him burned on the stove. The two men were reportedly beaten with a truncheon for two hours on the head, back, chest, arms, legs and genitals.

The police officer demanded US$50 from each of the prisoners. When they could not provide it, he took them to Tarlabaşı Police Station. There they were forced to strip naked. In turn they were taken to a small cell and forced to lie on their backs. The officer placed a chair over their legs and held the chair down. A junior police officer was ordered to pour cold water over the top part of their bodies. When they cried out they were beaten with blows so severe they reportedly drew blood.

Another officer appeared with a fire axe, the detainees were ordered to lay their genitals on a table surface and the officer threatened to cut off their penises with the axe. When the Ghanaians cried out, more officers appeared and this threat was withdrawn. The officer who had carried out the beatings reportedly made an attempt to rape one of the detainees, which was again interrupted by intervention by other officers. They were released that evening. A social worker who interviewed the two men five days after their ordeal confirmed that they had extensive bruises and swellings. There has been no investigation of their treatment.

No security for children

Most disturbing of all is the increase in cases of torture of children and young people detained on suspicion of minor offences. This is despite Turkey having signed the UN Convention on the Rights of the Child which prohibits the torture of children. Children from less advantaged social backgrounds seem to be particularly at risk.

In November 1994, 13-year-old Abdullah Salman was detained and tortured for three days on suspicion of stealing an envelope containing money and cheques from an owner of the Istanbul garment workshop where he was apprenticed. Although he protested his innocence, police allegedly resorted to torture to obtain a confession. Abdullah Salman described what happened:

> *"The Chief Superintendent said to me, 'Why do you tell lies, bastard', and began to hit me. He choked me and pushed me to the ground. While I was on the ground he hit my knees, and punched me twice.*
>
> *"Some time later they blindfolded me and trod on my hands. They took the sock off my left foot and tied something to it. Then they began to give me electric shocks. First I thought my toe had been cut off, then it was as if my body did not work from the waist down. Every now and then they hit my head. When I shouted out, those in the room shut my mouth and laughed."*

After three days of torture the police remembered that the Criminal Procedure Code stipulates that those detained for criminal offences must have access to legal counsel, and called a lawyer. When he saw Abdullah Salman's bruised body, the lawyer demanded a doctor. A medical examination at Şişli Forensic Medicine Institute found injuries which corroborated the boy's account of his treatment.

Abdullah Salman was released on 9 November. His mother, Şaziye Salman, made a formal complaint to the prosecutor. After some delay, and after she had been summoned to the police station and offered a bribe to drop the complaint, a prosecution was opened against a police superintendent. In pressing her complaint Şaziye Salman expressed the insecurity parents must feel: "If this happened to my son today, will it not happen to others tomorrow?" It is happening to others.

A 16-year-old girl detained in November 1995 told Amnesty International that she was repeatedly sexually abused after being detained by police officers who were looking for her brothers. She asked for her name to be withheld for fear that she would be arrested and tortured again. She was detained for 19 days and subjected to a variety of torture methods: given electric shocks, hosed with high-pressurized water, beaten and hanged by the arms for long periods:

> *"In the torture room I was given electric shocks to the vagina. They took a pen and jabbed it into my belly and breasts. They asked whether I was still a virgin and threatened to destroy my virginity so my fiancé would*

Even children are at risk of ill-treatment in Turkish police stations. Halil Ibrahim Okkalı* (above with his mother) *was placed in intensive care after police interrogated him in Izmir in November 1995.

> *leave me. Even though I told them again that I was a virgin, they accused me again of 'sleeping with terrorists'."*

Twelve-year-old Halil Ibrahim Okkalı was placed in intensive care with his arm in plaster after interrogation by police officers at Çınarlı Police Station in Izmir in November 1995. They had detained him on suspicion of theft. He said he was interrogated by two policemen who beat him with a truncheon and kicked him after he fell down. After he was released his father took him to Izmir Tepecik Hospital where he remained for three days. His injuries were confirmed by medical examination. On 28 November 1995 a complaint was filed with Izmir's public prosecutor on behalf of Halil Ibrahim Okkalı against the police officers, who went on trial for ill-treating a citizen at Izmir Criminal Court in March 1996.

Children's human rights are at even greater risk when they are accused of offences under the Anti-Terror Law. Lawyers are very often denied access to minors accused of such offences.

Incommunicado police detention of minors on any grounds, irrespective of whether torture is alleged, is unlawful under Turkish law and should be treated by prosecutors and the courts as a serious offence.[9]

In March 1996 the trial of 16 people — mostly teenage students — charged with membership of or having links with the DHKP-C began at Izmir State Security Court. Five school students, none of them older than 16, were among the 10 defendants held in Buca Closed Prison for up to three months before the trial began.

The juvenile defendants reported that during their detention between 26 December 1995 and 5 January 1996 at Manisa Police Headquarters they were blindfolded, stripped naked, hosed with cold water, and subjected to electric shocks to their bodies including their sexual organs. Male detainees were subjected to squeezing of the testicles and sexual assault with a truncheon; female detainees were threatened with rape and being subjected to gynaecological examination.

The trial of 16 young defendants charged with membership of the DHKP-C, which began in March 1996. They reported that during their detention in Manisa Police Headquarters they were blindfolded, stripped naked, hosed with cold water and subjected to electric shocks. One of the victims was 14 years old.

A 14-year-old boy, Mahir Göktaş, gave the following account:

"I had to undress ... They asked questions that were nothing to do with me; when I said I did not know they twisted my testicles. They said things like: 'That's it, your manhood is gone'. Four of them held me by the hands and arms and gave electric shocks to my right thumb, to my sexual organs, to my arms and to my stomach. Afterwards I had no feeling in my right foot and sexual organ."

A 17-year-old female had to be transferred to a hospital, because of vaginal bleeding following electric shocks applied to her genitals.

Sabri Ergül, member of parliament for the Republican People's Party, gave the following account of an unannounced visit to Manisa Police Headquarters:

"I heard a cry and opened the door of the next room to find out what was going on. The young people were there, they were blindfolded and some of them were naked. "

The children's torture testimonies are supported by medical reports from the hospitals where they had been treated during their detention. In June 1996, 10 police officers were indicted for ill-treatment and using torture to extract confessions.

Death in custody

In January 1995, 14-year-old Çetin Karakoyun was shot in the head while in custody at Mağazalar police station in Mersin. He died shortly afterwards in hospital. The authorities claimed the shooting was an accident which occurred when a police officer was "playing with his gun". Many detainees have described how police officers "play with their guns" by putting them to the heads or in the mouths of those they are interrogating. Çetin Karakoyun's father reported that the police had not given him an opportunity to see his son's body, but buried it in haste. The officer responsible was later arrested.

Detainees held under the Anti-Terror Law are at greater risk of torture, because they can be held longer in incommunicado detention and they have no right under Turkish law to access to legal counsel. The Anti-Terror Law has such wide scope that it is used daily to detain people who join non-violent demonstrations, work for legally authorized political parties, or write for legally authorized journals. People detained under the Anti-Terror Law not only frequently allege torture in police custody, they also frequently die in police custody as a result of torture.

In the six years to January 1996 more than 90 people died in custody, apparently as a result of torture by police or gendarmes. In most cases no official action has been taken against those responsible.

'Disappearance' — how to torture a whole family

Ten years ago people did not "disappear" in custody in Turkey. In 1991 there were a handful of reports, and several more in 1992. In 1993 there were at least 26. In 1994 there were more than 50 reported "disappearances", the highest number in any country reported that year to the UN Working Group on Enforced or Involuntary Disappearances, which expressed "particular concern at this considerable increase".[10] At least 35 people "disappeared" in 1995.

Most of the "disappeared" are Kurdish villagers with no history of political activity, detained during the course of security raids on suspicion of giving food or shelter to PKK members.

A deserted village in southeast Turkey. Hundreds of villages have been forcibly evacuated in brutal operations by government security forces marked by reports of extrajudicial executions and "disappearances". © R. Maro

Many families of the "disappeared" fear their relatives have died under torture, or that they were arbitrarily killed in reprisal for the deaths of soldiers in clashes with the PKK.

On 7 July 1994 the village of Akçayurt was forcibly evacuated following a clash between the PKK and the security forces. Villagers from Akçayurt and a number of neighbouring villages were taken to a containment area near the Topçular gendarmerie post.

While held at Topçular gendarmerie post, Mehmet Gürkan, the village headman, told television reporters that the PKK had burned his village. On his release a week later, he held a press conference retracting the statement made on television. He said that he had been tortured and that Akçayurt had in fact been burned by the security forces. He told a local newspaper:

> *"They took me to the Topçular gendarmerie post and tortured me. My ribs were broken. They collected the people outside the village and gave them nothing for four days ... 430 people of my village have now gone to Adana, Diyarbakır and nearby villages. We have nothing to eat. They also burned all of our crops."*

In August 1994 Mehmet Gürkan returned to the village to collect some remaining pieces of furniture from his home. According to eye-witnesses, he was detained by soldiers and taken away in a helicopter. He has not been seen since.

The relatives of Mehmet Şirin Maltu, a farmer, have had no news of him since he "disappeared" on 28 January 1995. Mehmet Şirin Maltu, from the village of Yanbüluk (Zediya), near Kozluk in Batman province, was detained by gendarmes. He was brought back to his family home the following day and a search was carried out using a metal detector. The Kozluk public prosecutor stated that Mehmet Şirin Maltu was never detained, but other detainees reported seeing him at Batman Gendarmerie Regimental Headquarters.

"Disappearances" also take place in the big cities of western Turkey such as Istanbul and Ankara. In March 1995 the body of Rıdvan Karakoç, missing since February and wanted by the police, was found on vacant ground in the Beykoz district and buried as that of an unidentified person. On 19 October 1995

Right: ***The wife and children of Fehmi Tosun who "disappeared" in October 1995. © Ş. Dayanan***

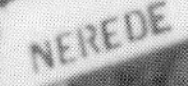
DÜZGÜN TEKİN
NEREDE
EHMİ TOSUN
9.10.1995' de GÖZALTINA ALINDI
KAYIP

Fehmi Tosun, who had previously been imprisoned for more than three years for alleged membership of the PKK, was abducted by three men carrying walkie-talkies, according to his wife and daughter who witnessed the abduction. He has not been seen since.

"Disappearance" is a human rights violation inflicted not only upon the victims but also upon their families. When someone "disappears", not knowing if they are alive or dead causes untold suffering to their relatives. Without knowing the fate of their loved ones people are suspended in uncertainty. In addition to this psychological trauma, the families of more than 100 people who have "disappeared" since 1991 have

Emine Ocak, shortly before being detained in Istanbul on 8 July 1995. She was among a group of families of the "disappeared" who had been demonstrating in Istanbul's Istiklal Street when police wielding truncheons broke up the protest. © Cumhuriyet

Right: *Mothers of the "disappeared" in Istanbul. Their sons Ismail Şahin and Düzgün Tekin "disappeared" in southeast Turkey and Istanbul respectively. © Ş. Dayanan*

been treated with a callous lack of concern by the authorities. "Disappearances" are continuing and those who "disappeared" in 1995 included three children. Relatives who have attempted to draw public attention to their plight have been subjected to ridicule and insults, beatings and detention by local security forces. Some have even been imprisoned.

Despite the authorities' obligation, under the UN Declaration on the Protection of All Persons from Enforced Disappearance, to have complaints of "disappearances" promptly, thoroughly and impartially investigated, Amnesty International knows of no such investigations in Turkey.

Extrajudicial execution in the southeast

Repression has long been the response to security problems in Turkey, but in 1991 certain elements in the security forces went even further. They stepped outside the law and began to wage a full-scale dirty war. An unprecedented wave of political murder swept through the southeast but continued onto the streets of Ankara and Istanbul.

Security forces make arrests in southeast Turkey. Blindfolding detainees is standard practice. The UN Special Rapporteur on extrajudicial, summary or arbitrary executions, in his 1995 report on Turkey, spoke of "a pattern of violations of the right to life, particularly against persons of Kurdish ethnic origin." © Rex

In the late 1980s Amnesty International had received occasional allegations of extrajudicial execution, but in the spring of 1991 the organization began to receive a large number of reports of "death squad" style killings of Kurdish villagers in the Midyat area of Şırnak province. The security forces were clearly involved in the killings. The perpetrators were able to pass through military check-points and were sometimes moved around using military vehicles or helicopters.

In mid-1991 Kurdish political leaders began to be targeted and by early 1992 scores of people were being gunned down in the first of hundreds of street killings by small groups of assassins in the cities of the southeast. In most cases the killers were never identified but there is evidence that the security forces were orchestrating the killings by arming and paying the assassins. Most of the victims were perceived by the security forces as potential enemies of the state. They were people who worked for left-wing or Kurdish nationalist publications, and people who had previously been detained or imprisoned on suspicion of membership of the PKK or other illegal Kurdish groups.

More than 1,000 people have died in these political street killings since 1991. One of those killed was torture victim Zeki Aksoy, who had pursued his torturers by exercising the right of every Turkish citizen and taking his complaint to the European Commission of Human Rights of the Council of Europe. He claimed that on 24 November 1992 he was taken to the Anti-Terror Branch of Mardin Police Headquarters where he was suspended by his wrists tied behind his back, kicked, slapped, and subjected to electric shocks to the genitals. On 26 October 1995 the Commission, on the basis of medical and other evidence, upheld his case and found that there had been infringements of his rights under Articles 3, 5 and 6 of the European Convention on Human Rights.[11] The judgment came too late for Zeki Aksoy. He was already dead. In April 1994 he told a Diyarbakır lawyer that he was being followed, and had received death threats by telephone. On 16 April 1994 he was lured from his workplace, a welding shop in Kızıltepe, Mardin province, and shot dead.

A former member of the PKK who had turned state's evidence later signed a confession to the killing. Zeki Aksoy's lawyer and family have questioned the validity of the confession, which was produced after Zeki Aksoy's complaint was deemed admissible by the Commission of Human Rights. They point out that the prisoner would be entitled to receive a reduced punishment under the Repentance Law and it might be to his advantage to accept responsibility.

Many victims were members of the People's Democratic Party (HADEP), a legally authorized parliamentary political party. HADEP opposes the use of political violence, but because its political goals to some extent resemble those of the PKK, the party is regarded in some quarters as the PKK's "parliamentary wing". Its predecessors, HEP and DEP, were closed down by the Constitutional Court for "separatism" in August 1993 and June 1994.

Legal sanctions have increasingly given way to political killing as a means of silencing those who oppose or question state policy towards the Kurdish minority. More than 100 officials and members of these parties have been shot dead since 1991. They include the member of parliament for Mardin, Mehmet Sincar, who was shot in Batman province on 4 September 1993. Other party members have "disappeared" and some have died in custody, apparently as a result of torture.

On the evening of 26 March 1994 Mehmet Şen, president of the local DEP branch, was seized from his café in Nizip, Gaziantep province, by plainclothes police officers. His wife, Nuray Şen, searched for him in every police station, but all relevant authorities denied any knowledge of Mehmet Şen's detention. Three days later she was informed that her husband's body was in Gaziantep State Hospital mortuary. The condition of the body suggested that he had been tortured before death. His head had been shattered on one side by a blow from a heavy object, and his right eye was out of its socket. All his fingers were broken, his right arm was broken, and his body was covered in bruises. He had been shot twice.

Nuray Şen is convinced he was killed in police custody. The official explanation of his death is that he was killed by unknown assailants. However, there is evidence which contradicts this account. Employees at Gaziantep State Hospital told Nuray Şen that her husband's body had been delivered to the morgue by four plainclothes police officers. Another DEP member was detained on the same day as Mehmet Şen but was later released. He said that while in custody he was told that Mehmet Şen was dead, and was threatened with the same fate. No investigation has ever taken place, to Amnesty International's knowledge.

One victim, who died in hospital after an armed attack, was able to tell relatives and hospital officials that he recognized his attackers as police officers. Muhsin Melik was a founder member of the Şanlıurfa branch of the HRA, the former president of Şanlıurfa DEP and a founder of the Şanlıurfa branch of HADEP. He and his chauffeur, Mehmet Ayyıldız, were attacked outside his office in Şanlıurfa in June 1994. Mehmet Ayyıldız was killed almost immediately. Muhsin Melik retaliated using a pistol which he was legally authorized to carry, but was fatally wounded. According to Muhsin Melik's family, he had received death threats from the security forces and in 1993 members of the security forces Special Operations Team had attempted to abduct him. In July the HRA published a statement made by Muhsin Melik in the presence of relatives and hospital staff:

> *"We got out of the car and the attackers immediately opened fire... I think there were four or five of them. They were using pistols and automatic weapons. I saw three of them very close up — I recognized them. Because they had been following me for a long time we had come face to face on a number of occasions. The people who shot me were people from the police team who were following me."*

Hüseyin Koku was president of the Elbistan branch of HADEP and a prominent critic of the local governor. In October 1994 the newspaper *Özgür Ülke* published a quote from Hüseyin Koku accusing the governor of using the security forces to harass and persecute HADEP members. The following day he was abducted by men in plain clothes. According to eye-witnesses, Hüseyin Koku was walking through the centre of town when he was stopped by men, apparently police officers, who made Hüseyin Koku get into their car. His wife, Fatma Koku, went straight to the police headquarters in Elbistan and says that the police confirmed that he was in detention. However, whenever she returned during the following days, the police denied holding her husband. The family then made inquiries at police stations in Afşin and Kahramanmaraş, but did not receive an official reply about Hüseyin Koku's whereabouts.

On 5 November Hüseyin Koku's family received a telephone call. The telephone was answered by his 13-year-old daughter. She first heard laughter, then recognized her father's voice

Hüseyin Koku was president of HADEP in Elbistan. In October 1994 he was abducted by men in plain clothes. His body was found six months later.

saying: "Do what you can to save me, they are going to kill me". Then there was the sound of crying or screaming. Hüseyin Koku's body was found some six months later, on 27 April 1995, near the town of Pütürge, in Malatya province, 150 kilometres from Elbistan. The body was in an advanced state of decay and the cause of death was not clear. On 28 April Hüseyin Koku's relatives identified the body at Pütürge State Hospital. Hüseyin Koku's body was transferred to the Istanbul Forensic Medicine Institute. It remained there until August 1995 when it was returned to the family for burial.

The Kurdish villager — only a pawn in their game

"If we go back to our village, we can feed our animals and look after our families. The government may allow us to go back, provided that we work for them as village guards. If we accept this the PKK terrorists will attack us, and if we don't the security forces will attack us. We just want the terrorists and the security forces to leave us alone. We just want to live a decent life."

Displaced Kurdish villager in Diyarbakır.[12]

Most victims of extrajudicial killings in rural areas are

Kurdish (or in some cases Assyrian) villagers who refuse to join the civil defence corps of village guards. The Turkish state has failed these villagers twice over. The village guard system was originally established as a result of the security forces' inability to protect villages from PKK attacks. Now the state is failing to protect the same villagers from burning, brutality and killing by the security forces.

In a conflict ranging over tens of thousands of square miles of rugged terrain, membership of the village guard system, or refusal to join it, is used by the government and the PKK as a method of holding down territory.

The system was established in the mid-1980s, so that village guards could defend their own village. Now, the 55,000 village guards form a paramilitary force deployed in operations against other villages and even incursions into northern Iraq, identification checks at road-blocks, and other duties, such as carrying out interrogations.

In theory membership of the village guard corps is voluntary, but in practice villagers face a terrible dilemma. While many are reluctant to serve as village guards for fear of being killed by the PKK, they know that those who refuse to join are subject to reprisals by the security forces, and village guards from neighbouring villages, who accuse them of supporting the PKK.

Security operations in villages are usually carried out by gendarmes, members of Special Operations Teams, and village guards, or all three acting together. The inhabitants of the village are assembled and those selected for interrogation are taken away to a police station, gendarmerie post or other place of detention, or are interrogated in the village itself. Unprotected by the most basic safeguards, they are often brutally tortured and killed.

An inhabitant of a village in Bitlis province, which had not joined the village guard system, survived an attempted extrajudicial execution in March 1994, but his brother and uncle were killed. The villager (whose name is withheld for his own safety) described what happened:

> *"At 7pm a group of armed men came to our village. They came to the centre of the village and assembled the villagers. They searched our village and they wanted us to show them PKK hideouts. They said that a group of PKK had come to our village and they asked where they were.*

We said that they had not come to the village... nothing like that had happened.

"They searched our houses... Then they took out a list, read out the names of three people — me, my brother and my uncle who was also the village headman. 'Show us the road to F... village', they said, and putting us in front of them, they took us straight to F... village. They took us to a piece of waste ground and then they opened fire on us. My brother and my uncle fell to the ground. I tried to escape [but] they began to fire at me...I threw myself face down on the ground. They shot at me again, and I was hit in the leg and in the back. I lay on the ground and pretended to be dead. They went back to the other two and fired a couple of shots from a handgun. Then they turned around and left."

The village of Budaklı (Kerşef) near Midyat in Mardin province did not participate in the village guard system. As a result it was repeatedly targeted by security forces. In May 1990 Beşir Algan, a farmer in Budaklı, was killed by one of a large force of gendarmes and commandos. In April 1995, following the murder by PKK members of the son of a village guards' leader in Midyat, village guards burned down several houses in Budaklı, and threatened to kill the villagers unless they became village guards. In May 1995 soldiers, accompanied by tanks and artillery, surrounded Budaklı, assembled the population in the village square, and detained 25 of them including the village headman. Twenty of the villagers were released that evening, at 6.30pm, and the other five were released some time later. All five were killed on their way back to the village, apparently by village guards. The names of the villagers were Ahmet Atuğ, Sükrü Demir, Abdulkadir Demir, Hüsnü Dilmen and Hetti Algan, a young woman whose body was found near a neighbouring village.

On 24 August 1995 Mehmet Nezir Akıncı, a minibus driver, was reportedly shot dead by members of the Special Operations Team in Budaklı village. On 31 August Osman Acar, another minibus driver and inhabitant of Budaklı, was allegedly shot by members of the Special Operations Team at a check-point near the village. The Midyat Public Prosecutor opened an investigation into the incident. On 25 August Budaklı was raided again by security forces and eight villagers detained for questioning following the funeral of Mehmet Nezir Akıncı. None of these extrajudicial executions has been subjected to impartial and expert investigation as recommended in the UN Principles on the Effective Prevention and Investigation of Extra-legal, Arbitrary and Summary Executions.

Hundreds of villages have been burned down in punitive raids by security forces since 1990.[13] Various sources estimate that as many as two million people have fled from their homes in the southeast over the past seven years, most of them as a result of forced village evacuations. The populations of Diyarbakır, Adana and Mersin are growing fast as villagers forced

A woman searches a rubbish dump for food in southeast Turkey. Two million people are estimated to have fled the violence in the countryside — many were forced to leave by security forces who burned or demolished their houses following forced village evacuation. Government provisions are inadequate and many displaced people live in temporary dwellings on waste land. © R. Maro

out of their homes and livelihoods flee to the relative safety of the cities. Government programs to deal with the influx have been quite inadequate and most of the displaced live with relatives in squalid, overcrowded conditions or congregate in temporary dwellings on waste land. An estimated 15,000 villagers who fled from settlements in Şırnak and Hakkari provinces allegedly after being subjected to aerial bombings and other attacks by security forces now live in a refugee camp in Northern Iraq.

Extrajudicial executions in Istanbul and Ankara

When the Turkish state resorts to illegal methods against armed opposition groups it puts the security of every Turkish citizen at risk. Since 1991, 87 people have been killed during raids on properties in Ankara, Istanbul and Adana, which police claimed were "safe houses" for armed opposition groups. Some of these houses were occupied by militants who opened fire on the police, but in many cases the circumstances surrounding the incidents suggest arbitrary killing by the security forces. Often the police gave no call to surrender, or made no attempt to place the premises under siege, but immediately opened up with automatic fire. Prisoners are almost never taken in such operations and important evidence, such as the victims' clothing, has often been "lost".

Mustafa Selçuk, Şirin Erol and Seyhan Akyıldız were killed in a police raid on a flat in the Kardelen district of Batıkent, Ankara on 12 April 1995. The police claimed that they were killed in an armed clash. However, a joint delegation of the HRA and the Progressive Jurists' Association examined the house and concluded, from the location of bullet holes in and around the property, that the three people had not fired shots from inside the flat, and that they had been captured before they were killed.

Comments made by the Justice Minister Mehmet Moğultay on 23 April 1995 show why extrajudicial executions should be of concern to all Turkish citizens: "People have been killed extrajudicially. Today, there are extrajudicial executions in our country. Unfortunately, these extrajudicial executions are carried out in every field of life — in schools, in families, in fields, on streets, in buses, among the press". Algan Hacaloğlu, State Minister for Human Rights, was more specific in a speech the following day: "There are extrajudicial executions in our country. The killing of the three people in Batıkent was examined by a delegation from my Ministry ... This is an extrajudicial execution. If it is not, the Interior Minister should demonstrate this by carrying out a deeper investigation." By June 1996 no prosecution had been opened.

Some of those killed in house raids were armed and met their deaths in the course of an armed clash, but in several cases, the victims were apparently ordinary Turkish people going about their daily business when they were suddenly caught in a hail of automatic arms fire.

Selma Çıtıak, a 22-year-old woman, worked as a cashier in a cafeteria in the Perpa shopping centre in Okmeydanı, Istanbul. She was killed on 13 August 1993 when members of a squad from the Anti-Terror Branch burst into the cafeteria and opened fire. Witnesses reportedly heard Selma Çıtıak call out: "Stop, I am coming out". Medical evidence supports the view that Selma Çıtıak was first wounded in the leg and was standing when she was shot a second time, in the chest. Three men, including Nebi Akyürek, the café owner, and Sabri Atılmış, a 16-year-old youth, were killed in the same operation. No police officers were wounded. Lawyers and independent doctors were not permitted to attend the preliminary post-mortems, in spite of the wishes of the families, and in breach of the UN Principles on the Effective Prevention and Investigation of Extra-legal, Arbitrary and Summary Executions.

Selma Çıtıak was married, with one child. Her husband, Nedim Çıtıak, strongly denied the suggestion that his wife had any connections with illegal organizations. Nebi Akyürek's brothers told the press: "Even supposing our brother was an anarchist, was the woman at the cash register an anarchist?" Nine police officers are currently on trial for the killings at Istanbul Criminal Court No 7.

3

Abuses by armed opposition groups

Illegal opposition groups which have turned to violence to pursue their political aims have killed unarmed civilians who took no part in the conflict. They have also killed their own members in the name of the party, Kurdish peasants in the name of liberation and Muslims in the name of Islam. Some of these groups have deliberately and arbitrarily killed non-combatant women, children and prisoners. Bombs and landmines have been used to maim and kill indiscriminately.

Amnesty International opposes the torture or killing of prisoners by members of armed opposition groups. It also campaigns against deliberate and arbitrary killing of people who have taken no part in the conflict and hostage-taking by such groups. Amnesty International works on behalf of those who are defenceless, including civilians and prisoners, and tries to influence governments and armed opposition groups to modify their treatment of those who are taking no part in the conflict.

Armed opposition groups responsible for human rights abuses include the PKK, the DHKP-C, the Turkish Revolutionary Communist Party (TIKB), the Turkish Liberation Army of Peasants and Workers (TIKKO) and the Islamic Raiders of the Big East-Front (IBDA-C). Of these, the PKK is responsible for most deliberate and arbitrary killings.

It is a bitter irony that during the 12 years in which the PKK has pursued its military objectives most victims of its deliberate and arbitrary killings have been Kurdish villagers. Reports from various sources show that armed PKK members killed at least 400 prisoners and civilians between 1993 and 1995. Most were killed because they had joined the government-armed village guard forces. Male village guards are frequently killed after being taken prisoner during PKK raids. Village guards Ramazan Baran and

Habib Kaya were apparently abducted by PKK members on 11 September 1995. They were found dead near Sarıbalta village, Tunceli province, the following morning.

Armed opposition groups have an obligation to respect basic humanitarian principles. Yet they knowingly put civilians at risk and have murdered others who took no part in the conflict. Since the conflict began, both sides have treated villagers in southeast Turkey as a soft target. In the 1980s the PKK frequently massacred whole families. Many women and children are caught in the cross-fire and killed in the course of armed clashes when the PKK attacks village guards in their villages, but relatives of village guards are also sometimes deliberately and arbitrarily killed. Eleven children were apparently deliberately killed when PKK members attacked the village of Daltepe, near Siirt, in October 1993. In the same month PKK members abducted 32 males, including six juveniles, from Yavi, in the Çat district of Erzurum, and killed them. In August 1995 the PKK reportedly returned to the Çat district, and abducted and killed Zülküf Kılıç and his two young brothers, Kadir, aged 16, and Halim, aged 13, from the village of Ağa.

In August 1994 a representative of the PKK told Amnesty International in a meeting in London that the organization had committed itself to abide by common Article 3 of the 1949 Geneva Conventions. This stipulates that people taking no active part in the hostilities, including members of the armed forces who have laid down their arms or who are out of action because of sickness, wounds, detention, or any other cause, must be treated humanely in all circumstances and should not be ill-treated or killed. Common Article 3 applies to all parties to an internal armed conflict, including armed opposition groups. The number of deliberate and arbitrary killings by the PKK fell after August 1994. However, Amnesty International continues to receive reports of such killings; there were 50 in 1995 and at least 16 in the first half of 1996.

Some individuals have been abducted and killed because they were suspected of being "collaborators" or "informers". Kurdish journalist Mecit Akgün went missing in mid-May 1992. His corpse was found on 31 May, suspended from a post near the village of Çölova, Nusaybin, in Mardin province. An autopsy

---

Right: ***One of the 32 men abducted and killed by PKK members in Yavi in October 1993. © Popperfoto***

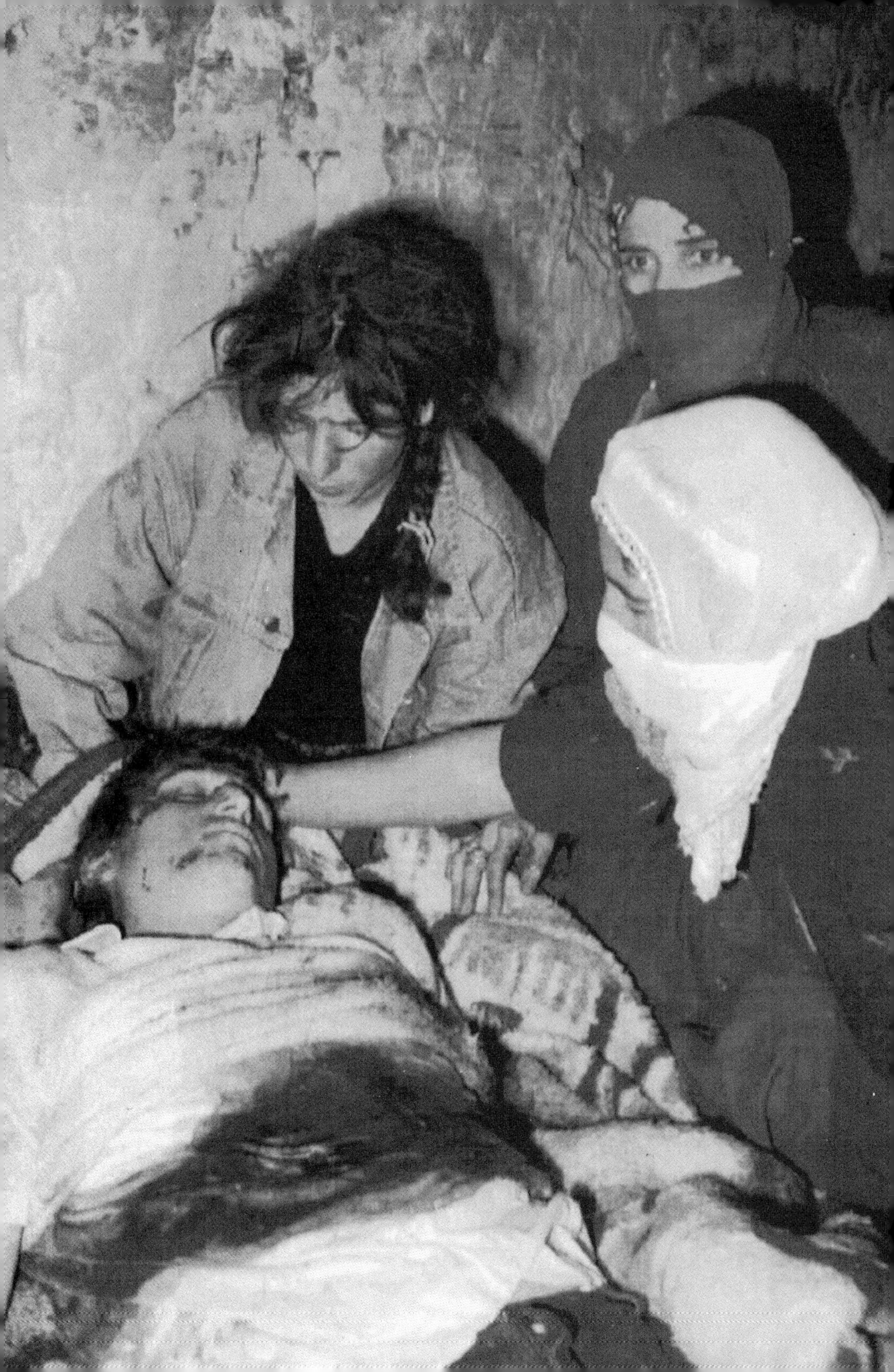

revealed that he had died of suffocation. A leaflet pinned to his body claimed responsibility in the name of the PKK. The leaflet stated: "He was punished for being a traitor". Common Article 3 prohibits the passing of sentences on people who are taking no active part in hostilities.

On 16 January 1995 armed members of the PKK carried out a raid on Erdemli village, in the Sason district of Batman province. They abducted Murat Yaşar, a shepherd, and Reşit Çoban. According to reports, Murat Yaşar was shot outside the village, while Reşit Çoban was brought back to his house. The PKK members opened fire on his house, killing Reşit Çoban, and wounding two members of his family.

There have been some allegations that prisoners have been tortured in PKK custody. On 14 January 1995, two Iranian Kurds, Asker Tahiroğlu and Zeya Nazım, were abducted and apparently interrogated under torture by the PKK before being shot. Their bodies, found on 29 January in woodland northwest of Istanbul, bore deep knife wounds; the ear lobes had been cut off.

Indiscriminate and other arbitrary killings

The PKK have also claimed responsibility for acts of indiscriminate violence in which civilians, including children, were killed and maimed.

In June 1993 they bombed the house of Mehmet Yalçın, a member of the Social Democratic Populist Party (SHP), in Suruç, near Şanlıurfa. Mehmet Yalçın's mother and his 10-year-old daughter Devran Yalçın were killed in the attack.

The PKK have planted bombs in public places, posing an indiscriminate threat to civilians. On 25 January 1994 a six-year-old girl, Gülistan Çelik, was killed by a bomb planted in the Diyarbakır governor's office. In the same month Ruhican Tul, a journalist on the *Turkish Daily News*, was killed by a bomb planted on a bus. In June 1994 Joanna Griffiths, a British citizen, died from injuries sustained in a bombing at a tourist resort for which the PKK claimed responsibility.

In March 1995 and again in April 1996, PKK leader Abdullah Öcalan publicly threatened that the organization would intensify bomb attacks on certain civilian targets in Turkey and abroad. While claiming to respect common Article 3 of the Geneva Conventions, the PKK has continued to execute captured village guards, while its declared intention to attack civilian targets suggests that, contrary to the assurances given to Amnesty International, the PKK would be prepared to resume indiscriminate killings of civilians.

Attacks on teachers

The PKK has treated teachers as a military target on the pretext that state education is delivered only in Turkish and that education in Kurdish is forbidden. Ninety teachers have been killed by the PKK since 1984. In late 1994 armed PKK members abducted and killed 19 teachers, most of whom were working in small villages in southeast Turkey. One of them was Ersoy Yorulmaz. On 10 October 1994 he and three other teachers in the area were taken to the nearby village of Düzköy where they were shot dead. His wife told the daily newspaper *Hürriyet* (Liberation):

> *"They knocked at our door at about 8.30pm. There were three people. They said 'This is Kurdistan, and you are acting as a teacher here. You must come with us, we have something to say'."*

Schoolchildren in southeast Turkey. Since 1984, 90 teachers have been arbitrarily killed by the PKK. © R. Maro

Selma Avcı awaits news of her teacher husband, Bekta Avcı, who has been missing since his abduction at gunpoint by the PKK in October 1993.

After strong public and international reaction the killings halted, but then on 28 October 1995 two more teachers, Ökkeş Kaya and Gürkan Arıturk, and Selim Korkmaz, a contractor, were captured and killed by the PKK near Dargeçit, in Mardin province.

The relatives of Bektaş Avcı, a teacher missing since he was abducted by the PKK in October 1993, are suffering the same anguish as the relatives of those who have "disappeared" in the custody of security forces. Bektaş Avcı's family have been seeking news of his fate since the night he was taken away at gunpoint. Bektaş Avcı was the principal of Yeniköy Middle School, near Bingöl, and was apparently abducted because he was a teacher. Amnesty International has received no reply to its repeated appeals to the PKK to release Bektaş Avcı. Three years after his abduction, his wife Selma Avcı told Amnesty International that her family has been deeply affected by the loss. She misses her husband:

"There are so many things I would like to share with him. Soon my son has to change school and I would like to discuss it with Bektaş. Even cooking meals is often very difficult, because it seems senseless to cook his favourite dishes without him being there..."

In a public response to a 1995 Amnesty International report in which arbitrary killings by the PKK were condemned, Ali Sapan, of the National Liberation Front of Kurdistan, the popular front established by the PKK, claimed that the villagers and teachers killed by the PKK were members of the MIT, the Turkish intelligence agency, or village guards, and that "the number of people killed is very limited". Killing of prisoners, irrespective of the crimes attributed to them, is a breach of standards the PKK has undertaken to observe. The deliberate killing of a single civilian or prisoner is one killing too many, but the PKK has killed hundreds of defenceless people and the killings continue.

Jury, judge and 'executioner'

The DHKP-C is an illegal left-wing organization which grew out of youth and student movements of the late 1960s. It began armed actions as *Devrimci Sol* (Revolutionary Left) in late 1975 and changed its name in 1994. The organization is based in Istanbul and Ankara, where it has carried out attacks on politicians, prosecutors, police officers and members of the security forces. It is also responsible for deliberate and arbitrary killings.

The DHKP-C frequently announces that it has "punished" a member of the public or a former member of its own organization for alleged collaboration with the security forces, and appears to consider such arbitrary killings justified in the interests of organizational discipline.

The DHKP-C was responsible for strangling Latife Ereren on 5 March 1995 at Istanbul's Sağmalcılar Prison. She was on remand on charges of DHKP-C membership and was apparently killed because the organization suspected she was an informer. The DHKP-C also killed Hasan Levent on 16 June 1995 in Istanbul because they believed he had given the police information about the whereabouts of a DHKP-C member who was later killed in a police raid.

Two high-school students, Emrah Sarıtaş and Engil Topal, were allegedly killed by the DHKP-C in the Alibeyköy district of Istanbul on 2 August 1995 because they were suspected of being informers. Tuncer Bağdatlıoğlu, a dentist, was killed by DHKP-C members at his clinic in the Içerenköy district of Izmir on 13 November 1995. In the 1980s he had been imprisoned and tried by the Istanbul Martial Law Court for membership of *Devrimci Sol*.

In January 1996 the DHKP-C carried out what they described as a "revenge" killing in retaliation for the beating to death of three prisoners remanded in Ümraniye prison on charges of DHKP-C membership. Several people entered the Istanbul business premises of the industrial conglomerate Sabancı Holdings and killed Özdemir Sabancı, a member of the owning family, Haluk Görgün, a director, and Nilgün Hasef, a secretary. The three victims were not responsible for, or even remotely connected with, the events at Ümraniye prison, but appear to have been selected arbitrarily by the DHKP-C.

The armed Islamist organization IBDA-C has claimed responsibility for several attacks, including some which have had lethal consequences for civilians. On 30 December 1994 a bomb blast in Istanbul's Marmara Café, Taksim Square, killed Yasemin Cebenoyan, a member of Turkey's Armenian minority, and Onat Kutlar, a writer and critic. In September 1995 the organization claimed responsibility for a bomb attack on Mathild Manukyan, the owner of a number of brothels in Istanbul and also a member of the Armenian minority, in which her driver, Necati Akça, and guard, Mehmet Urhan, were killed.

4

Bad laws and bad practices

When faced with incontrovertible evidence on a case of torture or extrajudicial execution, government ministers or ambassadors sometimes concede that there are "isolated cases" of human rights violations. But the government invariably denies that such abuses are practised systematically, emphasizing that responsibility must lie with the individual officers involved. Only rarely, however, are those officers prosecuted.

The truth is that, although individual officers must be held responsible for their actions, Turkey's persistent record of gross human rights violations results from a complete disregard at the highest level for international human rights standards and Turkey's own laws protecting human rights. These violations have been perpetuated by a deficient and flawed system characterized by unlawful, brutal and dishonest practices, supported and concealed by the Turkish state. Successive presidents, prime ministers and other high-ranking officials have all been fully informed of the violations and have failed to prevent, oppose or correct them.

The most frustrating aspect of Amnesty International's work on Turkey over three decades has been to see the factors which cause the high incidence of human rights violations persist unchanged. These factors have been the focus of Amnesty International's work on torture and they are now contributing to the increasing incidence of "disappearances" and extrajudicial executions. They are: extremely long periods of police detention; incommunicado interrogation; the concealment of abuse through false medical reports; official refusal to investigate allegations of human rights violations; the almost total impunity of the security forces responsible for violations; and a legal and judicial framework which sanctions these practices.

Prolonged incommunicado detention: an opportunity for abuse

It is widely recognized that lengthy incommunicado detention in police custody, especially before a detainee is brought before the courts, provides a prime opportunity for torture and can create the circumstances in which "disappearances" occur. The maximum detention period for people detained under the Anti-Terror Law is 30 days in the 10 provinces under state of emergency and 15 days in the rest of Turkey.

Not even those who advocate extended police detention in Turkey are able to offer a credible explanation of why police and gendarmes need to hold people for up to four weeks. Most detainees report that interrogation only takes place in the first few days. It is difficult to avoid the conclusion that long periods of detention are designed primarily to allow time for wounds inflicted by torture to heal.

As a safeguard against arbitrary detention, detainees have a right to have the grounds for their arrest promptly examined by a judge, under Article 5 (3) of the European Convention on Human Rights, to which Turkey is a party. An additional safeguard against arbitrary detention, torture and "disappearance" is found in Article 5 (4) of the European Convention on Human Rights, which states:

> *"Everyone who is deprived of his liberty by arrest or detention shall be entitled to take proceedings by which the lawfulness of his detention shall be decided speedily by a court and his release ordered if the detention is not lawful."*

Turkey has consistently failed to implement this guarantee. The Turkish authorities defend prolonged detention — as they defend so many institutions which violate human rights — on the grounds that it is necessary to combat terrorism. This argument was examined in detail by the Commission of Human Rights of the Council of Europe in October 1995.[14] While recognizing the emergency situation in southeast Turkey, the Commission questioned the necessity for prolonged detention without judicial control. It noted that there are no safeguards against torture in Turkey for prisoners held under the Anti-Terror Law, such as the remedy of *habeas corpus* or the right of access to lawyers, doctors, friends or family members.

> *"The individual may therefore, to a large extent, be cut off from the outside world for a period of time which can lend itself to abuse... In these circumstances, the Commission is of the opinion that, despite the serious terrorist threat in Turkey, the measure which [allows detention] for 14 days or more without being brought before a judge ... exceeded the Government's margin of appreciation and could not be said to be strictly required by the exigencies of the situation."*

The Turkish Government was unable to bring safeguards to the Commission's attention because there are none, and indeed Turkey has done nothing to implement the decision of the Commission. Detainees continue to be held incommunicado, at the mercy of their interrogators, for up to one month. They have no access to their lawyer, to a doctor, or to their relatives. When they are taken from their cells for interrogation, they are almost invariably blindfolded, making it difficult for them to identify their torturers.

The UN Special Rapporteur on torture has recommended that such incommunicado detention should be made illegal. This is because secrecy breeds torture and other abuses. Incommunicado detention hides evidence and excludes potential witnesses.

Detainees do not have free access to any medical practitioner, much less one of their own choosing, although this right is supposedly guaranteed under Rule 98 of the European Standard Minimum Rules for the Treatment of Prisoners. This is an effective method of concealing torture and makes it particularly difficult to provide medical evidence of sexual torture. In Turkey there are strong cultural inhibitions against reporting sexual torture. Nevertheless, Amnesty International frequently receives allegations from women of rape and insertion of objects into the vagina or anus, and from men of twisting of the testicles and insertion of objects in the anus.

During 1995 the Istanbul branch of the HRA received 12 complaints of sexual assault with a truncheon, 11 from men, and one from a woman. Six men and six women complained of threatened and attempted rape. Amnesty International monitored two earlier cases of alleged sexual torture, including rape

Turkey's laws are failing to protect her children. Twelve-year-old Döne Talun was detained for five days without access to her family or a lawyer on suspicion of committing a minor offence, and allegedly tortured.

with objects, in which the victims (both female nurses) were able to secure medical evidence. The prosecution of one police officer was blocked by the local governor's office, while the other case resulted in an acquittal.

Until 1992 all detainees had the right in theory to see a lawyer, but in practice this right was routinely denied. In November 1992 the right to a lawyer was formally withdrawn for those detained under the Anti-Terror Law, although it was retained for people charged with criminal offences.

When safeguards are ignored Turkish citizens can be exposed to gross abuses. Even children are not secure. All people detained for common criminal offences are supposed to be brought before a court after a maximum of 24 hours.[15] The Criminal Procedure Code requires children to be interrogated by a prosecutor in the presence of a lawyer. However, both provisions are sometimes ignored.

In January 1995, 12-year-old Döne Talun, detained on suspicion of stealing bread, was held for five days without access to family or legal counsel at Ankara Police Headquarters. She described what happened once she was in police custody, beyond the reach of the law:

"They beat me in the car as they were taking me to the police headquarters. In the evening I was blindfolded. They tied me up and connected a wire to my fingers. Then they said: 'We will give you something.' Then one of them switched on the generator. They also gave me shocks to my face. Next morning I was interrogated ... I told them that I didn't do it. One of them beat me with his walkie-talkie hard on the head. They also punched me in the stomach ... The bruising I had on my neck came from being hit with a truncheon."

When she was released, Döne Talun's family took her to the Forensic Medicine Institute and to the treatment centre of the Turkish Human Rights Foundation. A doctor examining her on behalf of the Turkish Human Rights Foundation found injuries consistent with her allegations of torture. The family made a complaint but a year later, the prosecutor issued a decision not to prosecute. Döne Talun asked Amnesty International: "How could they let them go, after what they have done to me?"

Until all detainees have full access to lawyers, doctors and relatives, police stations will remain fortresses of arbitrary state power, places of secrecy and fear where torture can be practised without any restraint.

Arbitrary detention practices, in which people are held unacknowledged for long periods, have also contributed to the rise of "disappearances". In southeast Turkey this is compounded by a persistent failure to promptly register detentions.[16] The UN Working Group on Enforced or Involuntary Disappearances drew attention to this in its 1995 report:

"Reportedly, procedures laid down in the Turkish Criminal Procedure Code for the prompt and proper registration and notification of their families are disregarded in the south-eastern provinces of Turkey. Furthermore, the lack of proper registration and notification is said to facilitate the disappearance of detainees."[17]

In recent years it has become almost standard practice for police to delay registration of detainees until several days after detention. This means that detainees' families suffer mental torment for days or even weeks while they contact lawyers, human rights associations and others in a desperate search for help. Families sometimes pay large sums in bribes in order to get confirmation that their son or daughter is in police custody.

A member of the Ankara Bar Association told Amnesty International in November 1994:

> *"People do not worry so much about torture nowadays – if your son or daughter just comes out of police detention alive, it is cause for rejoicing. Because police now habitually fail to register properly, every detention is a crisis – the Human Rights Association and lawyers are being worn down."*

In August 1995, after cases of "disappearance" in police custody began to provoke concern among the general public, the then General Director of Police, Mehmet Ağar, (now Justice Minister) announced that detention monitoring offices would be set up to track detainees. The Minister of the Interior, introducing the scheme, said that although the Criminal Procedure Code provided for relatives to be informed about detentions, citizens experienced considerable anxiety when family members were detained. The detention monitoring offices were to collect information about detentions and make it available to relatives and lawyers. Unfortunately, those offices that have been established have been largely ineffective because, as one lawyer explained, the various police units, particularly the Anti-Terror Branches, simply deny them information.

False medical reports

Suppression of medical evidence and the production of false medical reports are the next elements in the system which facilitates human rights violations such as torture and extrajudicial execution. On the last day of detention, most detainees are taken for medical examination by a state-appointed doctor. State-employed doctors can be put under enormous pressure to write "clean" reports for detainees who display medical evidence of torture. The Istanbul branch of the HRA, in its 1994 annual report on torture, documents no less than 29 examples of "clean" medical reports shown to be false by later reports documenting injuries.

Medical examinations often consist of no more than a quick glance at a fully-clothed patient at the other end of the room. A doctor in the State Hospital in Diyarbakır described his experience to a delegation of the Turkish Medical Association (TMA) in 1994:

"[The police] wanted a report from the State Hospital saying that no beating or pressure had been applied. I couldn't say 'Undress, I am going to examine you,' since that would be interpreted as me taking sides against them. Anyway, I started, carried out an examination, and the man had apparently been hung up. I confirmed this, gave my report and it was immediately torn up."[18]

Pressure is even put on detainees to participate in the cover-up. They are told that if they disclose their injuries to the doctor, they will be taken back to police headquarters for further "interrogation." But when a victim dares to reveal that he or she has been tortured, intimidation of the doctor can still ensure that evidence is suppressed. One female detainee who was examined at the Diyarbakır branch of the Forensic Medicine Institute in 1994 told Amnesty International:

"I was examined by a doctor. The police warned me not to say anything. But I did say that I had been tortured, and there were faint marks. He examined the marks but said, 'If I write it down, it will be hell for me'."

Usually the cover-up succeeds. Occasionally detainees are taken to prison in such poor condition that the prison authorities order a medical examination and the issuing of an accurate report in order to prevent themselves being held responsible for the injuries.

Doctors who resist police intimidation put themselves at risk. Mehmet Sıddık Doğru was detained by police in the Çorlu district of Tekirdağ, northwest Turkey, on 13 February 1996 on suspicion of membership of an illegal organization, and interrogated at Tekirdağ Police Headquarters. He claims that he was blindfolded, beaten, insulted and subjected to electric shocks. He was then taken by police to Cınarlı Health Centre in Tekirdağ where a medical certificate was issued stating that "there were no traces of blows on his body". After his release Mehmet Sıddık Doğru filed a complaint about his torture with the Çorlu Prosecutor. When examined by another doctor, authorized by the Forensic Medicine Institute, he was given a report stating that he would be unfit to work for 10 days. That same night Mehmet Sıddık Doğru was redetained and taken to Çorlu State Hospital where a "clean" report was issued. The Tekirdağ Police Chief told the local press:

"The doctors who gave the report [which described injuries] abused their professional status. They wanted to give the impression that there is systematic torture in order to subvert the course of justice and to undermine the security forces."

The public prosecutor opened an investigation against the doctors who had issued the report recording injuries, on the grounds that they had "humiliated the State by issuing a false report". Mehmet Sıddık Doğru applied to the Izmir Branch of the Turkish Human Rights Foundation where further tests were conducted. These tests corroborated his allegation.

Medical evidence is falsified or suppressed to cover up the causes of deaths in custody and extrajudicial executions. Legal representatives of families are sometimes denied access to autopsies and in many cases autopsy reports seem to contradict evidence that is plain to the family when it retrieves the body for burial.

Yücel Dolan, the 25-year-old son of the mayor of the town of Hazro, was arrested in July 1993 and taken to Diyarbakır Gendarmerie Headquarters for interrogation. Two days later his father Resul Dolan found his son's body in the morgue at Diyarbakır State Hospital. When washing the body for burial he says he saw evidence of beating on the lower legs, an injury to the back of the head and what appeared to be electricity burns on the legs and fingers. His son's genitals had been mutilated. Although an autopsy had been performed on Yücel Dolan, his family were not given the report. However, the public prosecutor told Resul Dolan that his son died of a heart attack.

In January 1991 Birtan Altunbaş, a medical student, died in hospital seven days after being detained and taken to Ankara Police Headquarters. An autopsy was performed but the results were never released. A fellow detainee reported that for four days and nights he heard Birtan Altunbaş's cries and saw him being made to run naked, supported between two policemen, up and down the corridor outside the cells, a method of diminishing the marks left by *falaka*. The government stated that Birtan Altunbaş died of "heart disease caused by malnutrition".

Even when there is medical evidence that detainees have suffered human rights violations, and doctors are prepared to face personal and professional risks in recording it, the judicial authorities frequently make no effort to investigate the allegations, let alone to find and prosecute the torturers.[19]

Failure of the judiciary

"What did you expect, sweets?" was reportedly the reaction of a judge to fisherman Kemal Gök's allegation that he had been tortured during interrogation at Izmir Police Headquarters in 1992. Judges and prosecutors who fail to investigate allegations of torture make up the next link in the torture system. The failure of judges and prosecutors to conduct such investigations is a breach not only of the state's obligations under international law, but also of the essential requirements of their profession.

Torture is a serious offence under Turkish law. Article 17 of Turkish Constitution states, "No one may be subjected to torture or ill-treatment". The Turkish Penal Code provides for sentences of up to five years' imprisonment for public officials found guilty of torture and between seven and 10 years when torture results in death.

International law, including Article 3 of the European Convention on Human Rights which by ratification has become part of Turkish domestic law, also forbids torture. Turkey is also a party to the UN Convention against Torture and Other Cruel, Inhuman or Degrading Treatment or Punishment. The Convention requires that reports of torture be promptly and impartially investigated.[20] However, many of Turkey's judges and prosecutors treat allegations of torture with a casual lack of concern which is in striking contrast to their diligence in prosecuting crimes against the Turkish state.

After medical checks, detainees are usually brought before a public prosecutor or, in the case of offences under the Anti-Terror Law, the State Security Court prosecutor. The detainees often refrain from mentioning torture at this stage, for fear of being taken back to the police station, but some do complain to the prosecutor. When Zülcihan Şahin, an 18-year-old student detained at the Anti-Terror Branch of Istanbul Police Headquarters in November 1995, told the prosecutor that she had been drenched with pressurized cold water, beaten, suspended by the arms, stripped naked, and subjected to various forms of sexual assault and verbal abuse, the prosecutor reportedly responded by smiling.

Dr Rifat Yüksekkaya was reportedly suspended by the arms and subjected to electric shocks to various parts of his body, including his genitals, at Istanbul Police Headquarters in June 1995. The Forensic Medicine Institute issued a medical report

Dr Rifat Yüksekkaya, who was reportedly suspended by the arms and given electric shocks at Istanbul Police Headquarters in June 1995.

describing several abrasions and "four dark lesions of about 0.2 cm in diameter on the tip of the penis". Dr Rifat Yüksekkaya filed a complaint with the Istanbul Public Prosecutor detailing the alleged torture, but has so far received no response. It appears that no investigation is being carried out.

Judges often fail to direct that allegations of torture be included in the court record. When they do, it is extremely rare for them to initiate investigations into those allegations, even when supported by medical evidence.

Amnesty International has received documents relating to the trial of five detainees — Mehmet Tanış, Nurgül Elveren, Sezai Gökmen, Gülhan Sezer, and Gülay Şaday — who were detained in June 1994 and accused of being members of TIKKO and participating in armed actions. When they appeared before Konya State Security Court they claimed that they had been subjected to torture and sexual assault during police interrogation in Tarsus and Konya. Four of the detainees who had made statements in police custody retracted them. Gülay Şaday reported that she had been given electric shocks on her feet, and that she still had bruises on her right wrist. It is entered in the court record that "as stated in the doctor's report, abrasion of the skin could be seen". The serial numbers of the police officers who carried out the interrogation appeared on the statements, but it appears that the judges did not initiate any investigation of the torture allegations in spite of the fact that evidence submitted to the court had allegedly been extracted under torture.

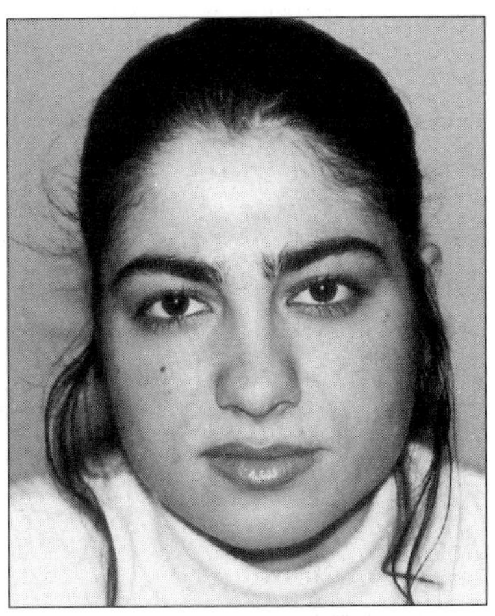

Journalist Mensure Yüksel Erdohan was interrogated at the Anti-Terror Branches of Edirne and Istanbul Police Headquarters in September 1995. She complained of torture to the prosecutor and the judge but this did not appear in the court records.

Mensure Yüksel Erdohan, a journalist, was detained on 24 September 1995 by gendarmes in Edirne, and later interrogated at the Anti-Terror Branches of Edirne and Istanbul Police Headquarters. According to her account, she was stripped naked, sexually assaulted and subjected to electric shocks. She complained of torture both to the prosecutor and the judge, but reportedly her complaints were not registered in the court record. She claims that the judge deliberately prevented her complaint from being noted in the file by interrupting her, stopping the court recorder and changing the subject.

Such gross negligence on the part of judges and prosecutors is not the exception, but the rule.

Impunity — state protection for torturers and murderers

State officials carry out torture, "disappearance" and extrajudicial execution and other gross violations because they know they will escape punishment. They are protected by police and gendarmerie officers of high rank, by prosecutors, by courts, by Turkish law itself, and by the silence of the international community. Prosecutions are very rarely opened against human rights violators even when there is strong evidence. The message to the perpetrators is clear.

It would not be true to say that human rights violators are never prosecuted. Prosecutions do take place, and there have been convictions. From time to time the Turkish authorities announce statistics on prosecutions of police officers for ill-treatment or torture, but have given no break-down of these figures, which do not seem to correspond with the very limited number reported in the media. From the available information it is apparent that the number of prosecutions opened into allegations of torture and extrajudicial execution is low, and the number of convictions lower still.[21] No prosecutions have been opened in respect of the more than 100 people who have "disappeared" in police custody since 1991.

In southeast Turkey prosecutions of police or gendarmerie officers are almost unknown. Those who can produce evidence of human rights violations and are willing to brave police threats and harassment face an additional barrier — the Law on the Prosecution of Civil Servants. This law, which was introduced as a temporary measure in 1913, gives local administrative councils established by the provincial governor power to decide whether to prosecute members of the security forces for any offence other than intentional killing.

The use of administrative councils to rule on whether or not prosecutions should be opened in response to formal complaints is a clear breach of the principle of separation of powers. Such decisions should only be taken by prosecutors and judges.

The administrative councils are comprised of members of the local executive who may have no legal background and may be open to influence from local security force commanders. In certain districts local commanders of the gendarmerie serve on the councils. Hearings are conducted in secret. Only if the administrative council decides that a case should be forwarded to a local

---

Right: ***Soldiers drive an armoured vehicle through Cizre in Şirnak province. Security forces have used similar vehicles to commit human rights violations with impunity. © Rex Features***

192

court are complainants and lawyers permitted to participate in the process. Complainants who have been called to testify to the administrative council have stated that they came away from the "hearing" (at which the complainant was not permitted to be accompanied by his or her lawyer) with the clear impression that the investigation was being handled by the local police.

Lawyers report that the administrative councils are used as a method of delaying proceedings almost indefinitely, as complaints of torture or ill-treatment referred to administrative councils can remain undealt with for months or years. Mediha Curabaz, a nurse, alleged that she had been raped with a truncheon adapted to deliver electric shocks while in detention at Adana Police Headquarters in August 1991. Her complaint, which was supported by medical evidence, was referred to an administrative council established by the office of the Adana Provincial Governor where it was apparently handled by a police investigator. On 2 January 1992 the council decided, on the basis of a report from the Investigating Chief Commissioner of Police, that the five police officers against whom the allegation was made should not be prosecuted "since it has not been possible to secure sufficient evidence that the suspects were guilty of ill-treatment". Mediha Curabaz's objection to the blocking of her complaint was rejected by the Administrative Court of Appeal. In response, she filed a civil suit for the injury she sustained in police custody. In June 1994 she won this case and was awarded a small sum in compensation, a breach of Article 14 (1) of the UN Convention against Torture, which requires the authorities to make "fair and adequate compensation" to victims of torture.

The most common official response to complaints of human rights violations is a blunt denial. It is claimed that detainees found dead in their cells have suffered "heart attacks", or injuries sustained while trying to escape. Appeals on cases of "disappearance" are dismissed with a few lines claiming that the victims were never detained, or may have fled abroad.

A typical example is the case of 11 men who "disappeared" from the village of Alaca, near Kulp in Diyarbakır, on 10 October 1993 after it had been raided by security forces. Turan Demir, Mehmet Şah Atala, Hasan Avar, Mehmet Şerif Avar, Mehmet Salih Akdeniz, Nusrettin Yerlikaya, Behçet Tutuş, Bahri Şimşek, Abdo Yamuk, Celil Aydoğdu, and Behçet Taç were taken into

---

Left: ***A gendarmerie post in Cizre. © Roger Hutchings/Network***

detention and held handcuffed under guard for 10 days in the village. Witnesses reported that on 20 October the men were forced into two helicopters and taken away. "Virtually the whole village saw the men being loaded into the helicopters", said one witness. "The village is now empty. It was burned down."

There has since been no news of the 11 men. In response to petitions, the Emergency Region Governor in Diyarbakır and the offices of the local prosecutor and of the State Security Court Prosecutor in Diyarbakır denied that the men were detained. In September 1994 Amnesty International received a reply on the case from the Turkish authorities which stated that the allegations concerning Mehmet Salih Akdeniz, Nusrettin Yerlikaya and Behçet Tutuş had been conveyed to the relevant authorities and that further information would be forwarded later. The remaining eight villagers had "not been detained at all, either on 10 October 1993 or before or after this date."

Trials are only opened in rare cases when public pressure develops on a case. Even then they usually end in acquittal or a sentence which in no way reflects the seriousness of the offence.

The trial of four gendarmes accused of torturing and killing Sıddık Bilgin took so long that the charges of torture lapsed as having run out of time before proceedings were completed. Sıddık Bilgin, a teacher in the village of Suveren, near Genç in Bingöl province, died in July 1985 during interrogation at the local gendarmerie post. The official explanation was that he had been shot while attempting to escape. After several members of parliament intervened, his body was exhumed from the yard of the gendarmerie post, where the gendarmes had buried him. The feet were reportedly tied together. Witnesses to the torture came forward and in 1987 a trial was opened at Ankara Criminal Court No. 2 against four gendarmes. In 1992 the four gendarmes were convicted of torturing Sıddık Bilgin to death and were each sentenced to a year's imprisonment and suspension from duties for three months. The sentences were quashed on appeal, and in April 1994 the defendants were finally acquitted. While the court accepted that torture had taken place, it ruled that Sıddık

---

Left: ***An interrogation room in a police station in Ankara. Detainees are usually blindfolded before being brought for questioning so they can not identify their interrogators. Council of Europe officials making unannounced visits to Turkish police stations have found equipment apparently used for torture. © Frans Hoeben/Hollandse Hoogte***

Bilgin had been shot while escaping. The charges of torture had meanwhile lapsed.

An example of the courts' extreme reluctance to convict police officers is demonstrated by the trial of three police officers dispersing a May Day demonstration in 1994. They were filmed and photographed severely beating Salman Kaya, a member of parliament. In May 1995 Ankara Criminal Court refused to admit the video tapes and photographs as evidence, and acquitted the officers on the grounds that there was insufficient evidence to convict.

Prosecutors and judges have failed to properly investigate most allegations of extrajudicial execution in Turkey. The UN Principles on the Effective Prevention and Investigation of Extra-legal, Arbitrary and Summary Executions requires that, where there are grounds for believing that an a extrajudicial execution has taken place, governments have a responsibility to establish impartial and expert commissions of investigation, with judicial powers to call and protect witnesses and to initiate prosecution. Since 1991 Amnesty International has repeatedly urged the government to establish such commissions. The Turkish authorities, however, remained apparently unconcerned by well-founded allegations of official involvement in the post-1991 wave of political killings, and were only forced to act in January 1993 (when the death toll was approaching 400) by public outrage at the assassination in Ankara of a prominent journalist, Uğur Mumcu. The Parliamentary Commission on Unsolved Political Killings was set up in February the same year. Composed of politicians rather than independent experts, the commission had no powers to protect witnesses, was inadequately resourced and reported great difficulty in obtaining documents and calling witnesses, who it said were being intimidated.

In April 1995 the Commission finally published its report. There had been more than 1,000 further political killings since the Commission was formed two years earlier. The Commission was clearly an unsatisfactory response to the scale of the killings it was supposed to investigate. Nevertheless, the Commission's findings were revealing. The report seeks to exonerate the security forces from any involvement in political killings, despite strong evidence to the contrary, while confirming serious illegal and improper practices by almost all authorities in the emergency region. The report describes an official cover-up of collusion between the gendarmerie and the illegal armed organization *Hizbullah*, an Islamist group, which has been held responsible for many political killings.[22] The report confirms that village guards and "confessors" (people who have turned state's evidence in exchange for a lighter sentence) are involved in lawless activities including killing and extortion; that "confessors" have been illegally released from prison to accompany the security forces on operations; and that crimes committed by "confessors" were covered up by public officials.

5

Turkey and the world

The question asked by many Turks is: what pressure, if any, is the international community bringing to bear on the Turkish Government to end the widespread abuse inflicted on its own citizens? The member states of the UN and the Council of Europe pretend to be pushing hard for progress on human rights and the Turkish Government pretends to be responding.

The governments of the international community have preferred to leave the protection of Turkish citizens' human rights entirely to the discretion of the Turkish state. Foreign governments are well informed about the extent of human rights violations in Turkey, through information supplied by their embassies and by human rights monitoring bodies of inter-governmental organizations, as well as by domestic and international non-governmental organizations.

Despite the urgency of the situation, however, the international community has been reluctant to turn expressions of concern into action. The Turkish Government, for its part, acts as if its appalling human rights record was no more than a public relations problem. This is illustrated by a statement from President Süleyman Demirel, reported in *Cumhuriyet* on 10 May 1995:

"In its foreign relations, Turkey is increasingly facing a human rights problem. If the problem continues to grow as it has until now, Turkey will begin to encounter very grave problems in its bilateral and multilateral relations, and these problems will begin to have repercussions in the economic and military spheres. Turkey's isolation in the outside world would mean, quite aside from new squeezes in the economy, the closing of foreign borrowing and investment potential and the reduction of income from tourism and exports. It would also mean that problems could arise in the procurement to meet our armed forces' requirements."

İNSAN HAKLARI
BEYANNAMESİ

Human rights are dealt with at the international level by foreign ministries and diplomats. Those ministries have a host of concerns other than human rights; they have little to gain and much to lose by pressing hard on their allies' human rights performance. While their job is to press the interests of their own nation, the main beneficiaries of human rights reform would be the citizens of Turkey, not their own. Nor are the records of their own governments without fault; in several European states Turkish migrant workers are not only victims of racial violence but also victims of racist ill-treatment by police.

There are other reasons why those nations who are best placed to influence the Turkish Government have failed to halt the deterioration in its human rights record of the past six years.

Perhaps the main reason why the key players in the international community take a benign attitude to human rights violations in Turkey is the country's strategic position as the border guard of the west. Throughout the Cold War period, Turkey was the NATO member nearest the Soviet Union. This was the key factor in muting international criticism of the military coup of 1980. After the establishment of the Islamic Republic in Iran, Turkey began to assume new importance for western governments as a buffer against militant Islam. Now, several years after the disintegration of the Soviet Union, Turkey is still regarded by these nations as a vital front-line ally whose situation — as a secular parliamentary democracy bordering so many potentially unstable regions — merits "special understanding" including, if necessary, turning a blind eye to infringements of fundamental freedoms.

There are other problems associated with tackling human rights violations in Turkey through international pressure. Many of the western governments in dialogue with the Turkish Government over human rights questions represent countries about which the Turkish public feel some reserve for cultural and historical reasons. These are largely Christian nations addressing a population of which the overwhelming majority are Muslim Further, the international community's failure to act effectively in situations of particular concern to many

---

Left: ***A child holds a copy of the Universal Declaration of Human Rights. Awareness of human rights issues is high in Turkey, particularly among young people, and public pressure for change is growing.***
© *Z. Aknar*/Cumhuriyet

Turks, such as the conflicts in the Former Yugoslavia and Chechnya, means that statements from these governments on human rights in Turkey are widely viewed as hypocrisy.

It is also not forgotten in Ankara that several European countries were responsible for a serious attempt to partition Turkey at the end of the First World War with Italian, French and British as well as Greek troops on Turkish soil. Throughout the 19th and early 20th centuries European countries raised what are now classified as human rights issues with the Ottoman Government and this repeatedly resulted in the breaking off of a part of the empire. The resentment at being lectured about human rights by nations who historically acted with very mixed motives is no doubt a factor in the Turkish Government's response to criticism.

There is also the "positive engagement" dilemma. Turkey is geographically a European state which manifestly aspires to closer integration with Europe. However, factors such as its predominantly Muslim population, its less developed economy, and its rivalry with neighbouring Greece, undeniably position Turkey on the fringe of Europe. There is growing realization in Turkey that full membership of the EU is probably many years away. This contributes to a current of political opinion, led by the Welfare Party (which scored the highest vote in the December 1995 elections), which talks about a future for Turkey in alignment with other Muslim nations, rather than as part of Europe.

Western governments justify their lack of resolute action by claiming that strong public condemnation of violations could drive Turkey out of dialogue on human rights, leading to a greater degree of unfettered abuses. The argument might be more credible if it were not used so readily by the Turkish Government itself, most recently by a spokesperson for the Turkish Foreign Ministry:

> *"In Turkey everyone is devoted to the deepening of democracy and human rights in line with the wishes of all the people in Turkey, and any pressure ... is likely to be counter-productive."*[23]

The role of the UN experts

While governments have failed to seriously address the human rights problem in Turkey, the expert human rights bodies of the

UN have performed their monitoring and reporting duties with thoroughness in the face of grudging cooperation, or downright refusal to cooperate, on the part of the Turkish Government.

The Turkish Government not only ignored the findings and recommendations of the ECPT and the UN Committee against Torture. In response to the UN Committee against Torture's 1993 decision on Amnesty International's communication, finding that torture is systematic, the government made an extraordinary public statement attempting to discredit the methods and impartiality of the Committee.[24]

The UN Special Rapporteur on extrajudicial, summary or arbitrary executions has documented the wave of alleged extrajudicial executions of the 1990s, and raised scores of allegations of such killings with the government. In his December 1994 report the Special Rapporteur stated that he remained:

African migrants, some of whom are recognized as refugees by UNHCR, living near the Iraqi border after Turkish officials attempted unsuccessfully to force them over the frontier. Turkey often fails to provide proper protection for asylum-seekers inside its borders. In 1996 Turkey returned Iranian asylum-seekers to Iran where they would be at risk of imprisonment, torture or extrajudicial execution. © R. Maro

> *"... concerned at the persistent and grave allegations of violations of the right to life in Turkey, particularly in the south-east of the country. For more than two years, the Special Rapporteur has found himself in the position where numerous allegations from a variety of credible sources and the replies provided by the Government, which invariably state that the killings are not of an extrajudicial, summary or arbitrary character, contradict each other."* [25]

In order to resolve these contradictions, the Special Rapporteur has repeatedly asked the Turkish Government for an invitation to visit Turkey, without success.

The UN Special Rapporteur on torture has for several years expressed concern at the continued practice of extended incommunicado detention in Turkey, and at the large number of allegations of torture which he receives. He has commented on the lack of detail in the government's replies, describing them as "unsubstantiated flat denials", and pointed out that this reinforces the pattern of impunity. "Most such replies risk being taken as a signal by those responsible for the torture of the Government's willingness to protect them and to have them continue the practice."[26] In his January 1996 report the Special Rapporteur notes that he has requested an invitation to visit the country but is still awaiting a response.

The Turkish Government has treated the UN Working Group on Arbitrary Detention with similar contempt. In April 1995 Amnesty International submitted the case of Selahattin Şimşek to the Working Group. Selahattin Şimşek , formerly a teacher, has been in prison since 1980 after severe torture and a grossly unfair trial by a military tribunal. He is now seeking a retrial. The Working Group forwarded his case to the Turkish Government in April 1995. The government failed to reply. In September 1995 the Working Group ruled that Selahattin Şimşek's imprisonment was arbitrary and requested the Turkish Government "to take the necessary steps to remedy the situation". No retrial has yet been ordered. The Turkish Government continues to ignore the recommendations of an intergovernmental body while Selahattin Şimşek enters his 16 year in prison. His current release date is 31 May 2000.

The UN Working Group on Enforced or Involuntary Disappearances has recorded the rise of "disappearance" in

Turkey and commented on the contributory factors, in particular the lack of proper registration of detainees. In 1995, after expressing "particular concern" that it had received more allegations of "disappearance" from Turkey than from any other country in 1994, the Working Group requested an invitation to visit and investigate the problem. By mid-1996 the Turkish Government had not replied to the Working Group's request.[27]

Governments fail to act

Human rights in Turkey are an international responsibility and a legitimate subject for international scrutiny. In the face of mounting evidence gathered by their own investigatory mechanisms, the governments of the UN have a clear duty to take the process further. For several years Amnesty International has urged the UN Commission on Human Rights to act on the findings and recommendations of the expert bodies. At the Commission's 1996 session political considerations again took precedence over long-standing human rights concerns; Turkey once more escaped close scrutiny.

Reluctance to take action at the governmental level is just as noticeable among members of the Organization for Security and Co-operation in Europe (OSCE) and the Council of Europe.

The OSCE (formerly the CSCE) is an intergovernmental organization encompassing all the states of western Europe, eastern and central Europe, Canada, the United States of America (USA) and Turkey. It has 53 participating states and deals with a range of issues including security and disarmament, human rights and cooperation on economic and environmental matters.

All OSCE member states have made detailed commitments to respect human rights. They have said that nothing — not even war or other security threats — can justify torture. They have reaffirmed that the right to speak and write one's mind is a fundamental right upon which many other rights depend. These are not legally binding commitments, but they are politically binding because member states have voluntarily accepted them. It is generally considered they should be no less binding in practice than treaties.

The OSCE does not condemn governments. It seeks to work with member states in a spirit of cooperation, but it has a collective duty to keep member states to their human rights commitments. It has manifestly failed to fulfil this duty. At the OSCE

Budapest Review Conference in November 1994 the EU group of countries combined with the Nordic group in support of a statement urging Turkey to invite an expert OSCE mission to investigate human rights. Turkey refused to engage in this process, and the governments of the OSCE failed to take the issue further by compelling Turkey to accept the mission, which they have the power to do.

The Council of Europe's monitoring body, the ECPT, has investigated and reported on the prevalence of torture in Turkey, but the Council's Committee of Ministers itself has taken no further action on human rights violations in Turkey for more than a decade.

It is possible that Council of Europe member states are hoping that the European Court of Human Rights will bring to bear the pressure that they themselves hold back from applying. Turkey has recognized the right of individual petition to the European Commission of Human Rights, established under the Council of Europe to deal with violations of the European Convention on Human Rights. People who have been tortured or who have lost relatives to extrajudicial execution, and human rights defenders who have taken testimony from dozens of families of the "disappeared", often express deep frustration that the outside world does nothing to help them. The international community appears to care no more than the Turkish state for the rule of law and this adds insult to their injury.

The right of personal petition, however, is unique in that it offers proper and legal evaluative and remedial processes which promise victims a conclusive result — a judgment and an appropriate level of compensation at the very least. The petition procedure has been increasingly taken up by victims of human rights violations in all parts of Turkey but particularly in the southeast. In 1994 former Justice Minister Seyfi Oktay commented on the possible consequences of the steady progress of cases through the system:

> *"Presently there are over 300 cases against Turkey at the European Commission of Human Rights. This figure is expected to increase. Because of the billions of liras in compensation these cases foresee, it is likely that a bill of trillions of liras will be presented to Turkey. Material considerations aside, the good reputation of the country incurs untold damage with every case ... The problems of*

the country cannot be overcome with palliative approaches and empty words."[28]

Two years on there are now more than 50 cases before the Commission. These cases and the few judgments already given might have been expected to prompt the government to undertake an urgent program of remedial action and reform. The Turkish Government has responded with palliative approaches and empty words.

Window-dressing

Foreign governments, reluctant to develop the good work of the UN Special Rapporteurs, the ECPT and other expert bodies, are keen to see token improvements in human rights protection which will excuse them from firm action. Successive Turkish governments have shown themselves very efficient at manufacturing such token gestures, including the ready ratification of human rights instruments whose provisions they subsequently ignore.

Turkish Embassies regularly circulate lists of "advances" in the field of human rights which contain a substantial entry on accession to international instruments. "On February 26, 1988 Turkey was the first Council of Europe member state to ratify the European Convention for the Prevention of Torture and Inhuman or Degrading Treatment or Punishment", states a circular issued by the Embassy in Stockholm in November 1995, not mentioning that Turkey has vetoed publication of reports prepared under the terms of that Convention. The circular continues: "On August 2, 1988 Turkey became party to the UN Convention against Torture and Other Cruel, Inhuman or Degrading Treatment or Punishment", but it does not repeat the finding of the UN Committee against Torture that torture is "systematic" in Turkey. The recommendations for the prevention of torture emerging from both treaty bodies have not been implemented in any respect by Turkish governments.

Establishing cosmetic human rights bodies is another favourite tactic. In December 1990 the government established the Parliamentary Human Rights Commission. A Ministry of State for Human Rights was created in 1991. In September 1993 a High Council for Human Rights and an Under-secretaryship for Human Rights were established under the Prime Minister's office.

The suspicion that these watchdogs were intended as window-dressing is confirmed by the fact that as each of these bodies began to grow teeth and take its mission seriously, it was abolished. The transformation of human rights ministers into outspoken human rights defenders was one of the more heartening spectacles of the past six years. Azimet Köylüoğlu began his duties with the type of gesture with which the Turkish authorities seem comfortable: presenting framed copies of the Universal Declaration of Human Rights to police chiefs. He later began to criticize the behaviour of the security forces in increasingly strong terms. Not long after describing village burnings in the Tunceli area in 1994 as "state terror", he was reshuffled and replaced by Algan Hacaloğlu who eventually proved an ardent advocate of reform who spoke publicly with convincing passion about "disappearances" and extrajudicial executions. He was replaced in the lead up to the elections of December 1996.

In late 1994 the High Council for Human Rights produced a thorough report on the practice of torture, which it described as widespread and systematic, and made recommendations for legislative and administrative reforms to prevent it. The legislative measures included reducing detention periods to a maximum of four days, and giving all detainees access to lawyers. The report became available in May 1995 but was never publicized, far less acted upon.

The Human Rights Ministry was abolished by the new government in March 1996, and the High Council for Human Rights no longer functions.

The latest development in human rights bureaucracy graphically illustrates the state's approach to the problem. The founding of the Human Rights and Foreign Relations Directorate was announced in February 1996. Its duties are described as "combating allegations of human rights violations made with the intention of undermining the security forces".

In the interests of national security?

Foreign governments frequently justify their soft line on human rights violations in Turkey on the grounds that the government and the security forces face violent armed opposition. The Turkish Government unashamedly exploits PKK abuses to counter criticism of, or justify, its own violations. The Foreign Ministry regularly produces bulletins listing PKK atrocities, and circulates magazines containing photographs of villagers allegedly murdered by the PKK to European governments. These magazines are also sent to people outside Turkey who have sent appeals to the government on behalf of villagers believed to be at risk of torture or "disappearance". The UN Special Rapporteurs and Working Groups note in their reports that the Turkish Government encloses similar publications with its brief and unsatisfactory responses to inquiries about allegations of torture and "disappearance" of Turkish citizens.

Ömer Vehbi Hatipoğlu, *Refah* Party member of parliament for Diyarbakır, drew attention to the disingenuousness of such responses on the part of the government:

> *"Turkey is not a police state, it is a state under the rule of law. Thousands have also been killed in unsolved political murders. There are those who come to the podium and say 'Why don't you mention the PKK?' Members of parliament do not talk to the PKK. We address the government, not the PKK."*[29]

The Turkish Government tries to discredit its critics at home and abroad by suggesting that they sympathize or collude with the PKK. In response to an urgent appeal issued by Amnesty International for the release of three teachers abducted by the PKK, the Turkish Government issued an extraordinary public statement, claiming that "Amnesty International is in fact conducting an indirect campaign in support of the PKK".[30] They had reached this conclusion on the basis that, by describing events in southeast Turkey as "a conflict" and calling on the government and the PKK to respect common Article 3 of the Geneva Conventions, Amnesty International intended to give the PKK special status as a "warring party" under international humanitarian law.[31] Similar unfounded accusations of partiality and even outright collaboration with the PKK have been directed at other domestic and international human rights organizations. On this basis, Amnesty International delegates, critical journalists and politicians have been denied access to Turkey.

In opposing abuses by armed opposition groups Amnesty International neither supports nor condemns the resort to violence by opposition groups. Amnesty International is simply asking these groups to abide by provisions of humanitarian law to which they are bound and which they have pledged to respect. Citing these provisions is not a statement of position on the legitimacy or status of the groups, or of the conflict.

The Turkish Government would also like to gag critics of its human rights record at international governmental meetings. In May 1995, after critical resolutions had been passed in the Parliamentary Assembly of the Council of Europe and the European Parliament, Foreign Minister Erdal Inönü spoke disapprovingly of "the fashion to scrutinize the level of democracy in each country. The principle of human rights has taken precedence over another important principle — that of not interfering in the internal affairs of other states". He went on to describe the attitude of the Parliamentary Assembly and the European Parliament towards Turkey as "offensive and separatist".[32]

The Turkish Government has refused to invite the OSCE, or the UN Special Rapporteurs and Working Groups to visit the country, and when individual representatives make uninvited visits they can expect a strong reaction. In June 1995 State Minister Ayvaz Gökdemir publicly described three female members of the European Parliament who visited Turkey to investigate human rights violations as "these whores coming from Europe". Ayvaz Gökdemir was not asked to resign; he was reappointed to the cabinet of the new coalition government in March 1996.

In summary, the international community is well aware of the extent of human rights violations in Turkey but has shown itself too ready to collude with the Turkish Government in minimising the problems or finding excuses for inaction. Most governments would agree in principle with the proposition that ignoring human rights violations only stores up greater security problems for the future. Amnesty International believes that Turkey's allies have a responsibility to be firm in addressing human rights issues, a duty which they are currently failing to fulfil. Those countries which are involved in security cooperation or the transfer of military or security equipment or expertise have a special responsibility.

Military, security and police transfers

Amnesty International takes no stand on the legitimacy of military or security relations with countries where human rights are violated, but opposes the transfer of military, security or police equipment, personnel, training or logistical support, whenever it has reason to believe that such transfers contribute directly to human rights violations. Recent reports indicate that some types of military and security equipment supplied to Turkey may have been specifically used by the Turkish security forces to commit such violations.

In October 1994 Turkish security forces burned 17 villages around Tunceli in eastern Turkey during a three-week offensive against the PKK. The *Reuters* news agency reported that US-made Sikorsky and Super Cobra helicopters flew over Tunceli town that day, ferrying in troops and launching rocket attacks.

During these operations Ali Karaca, a miller from the village of İbnimahmut was reportedly detained. A relative told the Kurdish-owned newspaper *Özgür Ülke*:

> *"Soldiers attached to Ataçınarı Gendarmerie Post carried out a security raid on the district ... They tortured Ali Karaca near his house. Then they called a helicopter by radio, put him in the helicopter and took him first to Ataçınarı Gendarmerie Post, and then to Tunceli. We found him at Tunceli State Hospital. His condition was serious, so we moved him to Elazığ State Hospital. After three days in a coma, he died ... At the hospital they first told us that there were signs of blows on his body, and that he had died of blows to the head. Then the soldiers intervened, and then the hospital said that he had died of meningitis and high blood pressure. They did not give us the X-rays."*[33]

Amnesty International has received several reports of the use of helicopters and other aircraft when human rights violations were committed. Helicopters were reportedly used to ferry troops in village raids in which "disappearances" occurred — for example, the "disappearance" on 24 May 1994 of the brothers Mehmet Selim Örhan, Hasan Örhan and Cezair Örhan, who were detained in Deveboyu village near Kulp in Diyarbakır province by soldiers from Bolu Commando Brigade, supported by helicopters. On 26 March 1994 several villages in Şırnak were bombed, reportedly by jet aircraft, resulting in the killing of at least 17 children. Officials claimed the bombing was accidental, but local inhabitants said that just days before the bombing they had been subjected to death threats from security forces for refusing to join the village guards.

Ali Ihsan Dağlı, captured by gendarmes at Kuruçayır village in Diyarbakır province, reportedly "disappeared" after being taken away for interrogation in a helicopter in April 1995. In May Amnesty International wrote to the Turkish Interior Minister about the "disappearance", urging an investigation into the whereabouts of Ali Ihsan Dağlı, but by June 1996 had received no reply indicating his whereabouts.

In January 1995 Amnesty International called for an immediate cessation of all sales or transfers of military helicopters to the Turkish Government. France, Germany, Italy, Russia and the USA have, in the 1990s, sold military transport, surveillance and attack helicopters to Turkey.

In August 1994 a Turkish defence industry spokesperson stated that Turkey had received 45 US-built Sikorsky Black Hawk military helicopters by the end of 1993. A co-production deal involving 50 more such helicopters was due to start in 1994, but has been suspended "in the light of helicopter purchases from Italy and Russia". In November 1992 the Turkish Government signed an agreement with the Russian Federation to import an undisclosed number of multipurpose Mi-17 transport helicopters. According to the UN Register of Conventional Arms for 1993 and 1994, the only country which provided Turkey with military helicopters equipped with integrated air-to-surface weapons was the USA, which supplied 31 attack helicopters. These included Super Cobra helicopters. It is also reported that a joint Franco-German company, Eurocopter, will begin delivery of multipurpose Puma helicopters to Turkey in 1996 or 1997.

Other types of military equipment provided by foreign countries to Turkey may have also been used by the Turkish security forces to commit serious human rights violations. For example, on 21 March 1993 security forces were filmed driving an armoured personnel carrier into a crowd in the town of Cizre and shooting at people gathered on a roof. The soldiers were shown striking an unarmed man with the butts of their weapons and beating his head against the vehicle before driving away with him. The vehicle used in this operation is believed to be a US-built Cadillac-Gage V-150 Commando armoured combat vehicle.

Left: ***Soldiers board a helicopter in the mountains in southeast Turkey. There is evidence that military helicopters manufactured outside Turkey have been used to commit human rights violations, especially in remote villages.***
© Popperfoto

Turkey bought 74 Cadillac-Gage armoured vehicles from the USA in 1993.

Izzet Tuğal was last seen alive being taken away in an armoured vehicle. He was found dead on 20 December 1995, one month after being taken into custody. He was visiting his parents in the village of Çavundur (Licok), near Lice in Diyarbakır province when he was abducted by five men wearing similar clothing to that worn by the PKK and carrying walkie-talkies and Kalashnikovs. When Izzet Tuğal's mother asked where they were taking him, they told her they were going to take a statement from him. Izzet Tuğal's father followed them to a place half way between Çavundur and the neighbouring village of Boyunlu where he saw two armoured vehicles, two military trucks and 10 soldiers waiting. Izzet Tuğal and the other five got into these vehicles which drove away.

The family applied to Diyarbakır State Security Court and Lice Public Prosecutor for information concerning the whereabouts of their son, but the authorities denied he was in custody. Then on 20 December, news came that Izzet Tuğal's body had been found near Boyunlu village. When the family went to collect the body, they found that he had been tortured. His left foot

Armoured vehicles have been used to commit serious human rights violations in southeast Turkey. In December 1995 Izzet Tuğal was reportedly abducted by five men with an armoured vehicle escort. His body was found a month later. © Hollandse Hoogte

Izzet Tuğal

was broken in two places, his jaw was broken and there were bruises under his eyes.

The USA supplied 250 armoured combat vehicles to Turkey during 1992 and 1993, while Germany supplied 187 and the Russian Federation supplied 115 during the same period.[34] Turkey now co-produces an "armoured infantry fighting vehicle" with parts from the USA and France. Since 1987 a Turkish company has assembled Land Rovers under licence from the UK parent company for sale to the military and civilian markets in Turkey. In June 1994 production began in Turkey of a new type of Land Rover, using imported automotive parts, and designed for transporting troops for counter-insurgency and light attack. About 2,500 will be assembled every year for use by the Turkish army and security forces. The new vehicle was tested in both the UK and Turkey.

Bedri Tan, headman of the village of Kadıköy (Qadiya) was found dead after being detained and driven away in a gendarmerie Land Rover. He was detained at his home by gendarmes from the Diyarbakır Regimental Gendarmerie Headquarters and the Hani Gendarmerie Headquarters on 13 September 1994. According to his family, he was taken into a separate room in the house, interrogated under torture, and taken away in a gendarmerie Land Rover. On 14 September Bedri Tan's family received a telephone call from Hani Gendarmerie Headquarters telling them to collect his body. When they arrived at the Gendarmerie they were shown the body in a bag in the courtyard. The upper half of the body had been dismembered. According to the gendarmes, Bedri Tan had been killed by a landmine while showing them the location of a PKK hide-out. According to his family, Bedri Tan had no previous involvement in politics and had never been detained before.

Companies in Belgium, France, Germany, Israel and the USA submitted bids to supply 350,000 modern assault rifles to replace the old rifles used by Turkish gendarmes and police.

Amnesty International is concerned by reports that military and security equipment transferred to the Turkish Government contributes to the commission of human rights violations by the Turkish security forces. Such transfers should be prohibited unless it can be demonstrated by the Turkish and supplying governments that they will not facilitate human rights violations such as "disappearances", extrajudicial executions and torture. This was the spirit of the recommendation adopted on 24 November 1993 by the Special Committee of the OSCE Forum for Security Co-operation, which states:

> *"Each participating State will avoid transfers which would be likely to be used for the violation or suppression of human rights and fundamental freedoms."*[35]

6

Reform a step away

There are many economic, social and cultural factors which will work strongly in favour of speedy and effective reform when the Turkish Government demonstrates the political will to put an end to torture and other state abuses.

Turkey is a modern, relatively wealthy country with many of the institutions and traditions necessary to sustain respect for human rights. Its well-developed infrastructure would enable reforms to be quickly enacted. Turkey has a comprehensive system of local courts, judges and prosecutors with at least formal independence from the state. Every province has a local bar association, some of which have demonstrated resolute independence by protesting against abuses and campaigning for the protection of the right of defence.

Although Turkey's recent political history has been repeatedly interrupted by military interventions, there has also been nearly a half century of multi-party democracy, during which time parliamentary government has become firmly established. Some members of parliament are prepared to voice strong criticism of the government and even the military on human rights issues.

The Turkish media enjoys considerable freedom. Sections of the media provide an effective watchdog on the worst of state abuses. Human rights are a talking point in Turkey and there is no doubt that broad sectors of the media are ready and willing to welcome positive change while others are capable of seriously and accurately monitoring progress.

It may be due to the tolerance of large sections of Turkish society that, although the bitter political struggles of the past 20 years have had a clear ethnic and sectarian dimension, there is relatively little intercommunal violence between ordinary people of Turkish and Kurdish ethnicity, or between Alevi and conventional Sunni believers. The security forces may target smaller ethnic and religious groupings in society — including Alevis, Assyrian Christians, Yezidis, Kurds, African and Iranian migrants and asylum-seekers — but this is not a pattern widely reflected in civil society.

None of the main legal or illegal political parties are promoting racial hatred. In the weeks following the general election of October 1991, when a new government was making promises on human rights and reconciliation, the wave of optimism which swept Turkey demonstrated that people were not only tired of conflict but eager to move their society onto a new footing. Nobody in public life questioned the desirability or achievability of harmony between citizens of Turkish and Kurdish ethnicity.

Past progress

Although the general picture for basic human rights in Turkey in the 1990s has been one of swift deterioration, progress has been made in some areas.

Perhaps most importantly, on 25 October 1994 Turkey joined the community of states who have abandoned the use of the death penalty. Although the death penalty is retained in law in Turkey and courts are still imposing death sentences, the Turkish parliament has not only held back from sanctioning executions (on which it has the final vote) but has also reduced the number of capital offences and commuted all death sentences for crimes committed before April 1991.

Threats to resume executions have met strong public and parliamentary opposition. Several former ministers have spoken out strongly against the death penalty, as have members of the Turkish judiciary. Retired military prosecutor and judge Colonel Nejat Öztaşkent said:

> *"The state should not kill ... I want the death penalty removed from the Turkish Penal Code. Those who give judgment are human beings and can make mistakes. Nobody can claim that all death sentences have been given justly. Once an execution has taken place, it is impossible to remedy a mistake. It is wrong to think that an unhealable wound should be opened by the state."*[36]

The death penalty is an issue over which Turkish civil society has taken a stand. After a lengthy trial for urging the government to abolish the death penalty in 1985, six members of the executive committee of the TMA were eventually acquitted. The TMA finally issued a code of ethics which prohibited Turkish doctors from providing medical services at executions (the Turkish Criminal Procedure Code requires a doctor to be present at an execution). In December 1993 the TMA stated:

> *"We believe that an end must be put to the paradoxical situation whereby those whose duty it is to maintain life take part in the act of killing. We, the members of the Central Council of the TMA, declare that, should we be required to participate in an execution, we will under no circumstances accept such a request."*

The TMA has also documented and publicized the problems of doctors under pressure from the security forces to issue false medical certificates and autopsy reports, particularly in provinces under state of emergency. The TMA has disciplined doctors who have falsified medical evidence, but it has also supported medical practitioners faced with what a Council of Europe report called "The intolerable choice between complicity and heroism — between the side of the torturers and that of the victims."[37]

Simple steps can save lives

Further important but quite uncontroversial changes are long overdue. An example of a simple step which could have saved the lives of nine prisoners beaten to death since 1994 would be to ensure that remand and convicted prisoners are never brought into contact with police and gendarmes. Once a prisoner is formally arrested by a court they pass from the authority of the Interior Ministry (police) into that of the Justice Ministry (prison service).

There does not appear to be a pattern of systematic torture in Turkish prisons. However, there have been many reports of vicious beatings and other ill-treatment of political prisoners when they are being transported by gendarmes for trial or medical treatment, or alternatively, when gendarmes and police are brought into prisons to quell prisoners' protests. Police and gendarmes take these opportunities to "punish" alleged or convicted members of illegal armed organizations.

In September 1995 political prisoners in Ward 6 at Buca Prison, near Izmir, refused to appear for roll-call in protest at

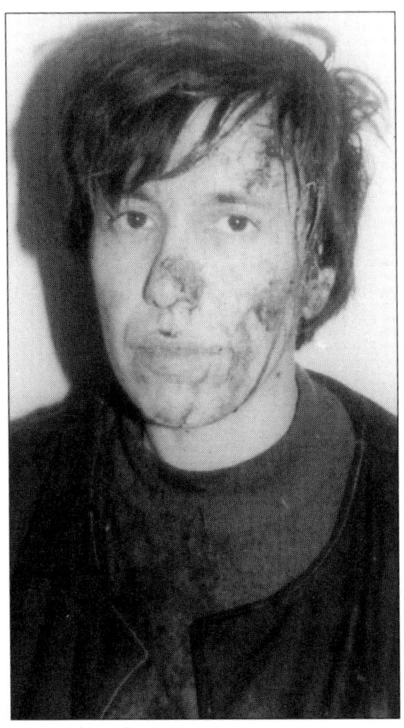

A simple change like moving responsibility for transport of prisoners from Interior to Justice Ministry could prevent attacks like that allegedly suffered by Hayriye Gündüz who complained that she was very severely beaten by gendarmes who were guarding her at Istanbul State Security Court in October 1994. She made an official complaint but the prosecutor took no action.

brutal treatment by gendarmes while being taken to and from court. A large force of gendarmes forced entry into Ward 6. After subduing the prisoners, the gendarmes allegedly brought them into the courtyard one by one and beat them savagely with chains, iron bars, sticks and truncheons. A prisoner held in a neighbouring ward gave the following account:

"There was no sound from those prisoners thrown into the courtyard. You could only hear their gasping. They were beaten on their heads. The courtyard was awash with blood which was on the walls and even the ceiling."

Three prisoners, Yusuf Bağ, Uğur Sarıaslan and Turan Kılınç, were beaten to death. The injuries documented in Turan Kılınç's autopsy report suggested a ferocious attack: "general body trauma, broken skull, subdural and subarachnoidal haemorrhage, broken ribs, laceration and haemorrhage of the left lung."

A few months after this incident, in January 1996, Orhan Özen, Rıza Boybaş and Abdülmecit Seçkin were beaten to death, and Gültekin Beyhan died later in hospital from head injuries, after police and gendarmes entered Ümraniye Special Type Prison to subdue a political prisoners' protest.

These and many other incidents, several of which have resulted in fatalities, show that gendarmes and police, who may be deployed in operations against armed opposition groups, should not have contact with prisoners charged with membership of such groups — particularly at times of heightened tension such as during a prison riot. Guarding and management of prisoners who have been arrested or convicted by courts should be restricted to Justice Ministry personnel.

For several years Amnesty International has called for simple reforms that could secure fundamental change. Turkey is well placed to enact reform; there is growing pressure on human rights issues from civil society and growing interest in these issues from the Turkish public. Since it would take only a series of simple steps to secure fundamental reform, why has there

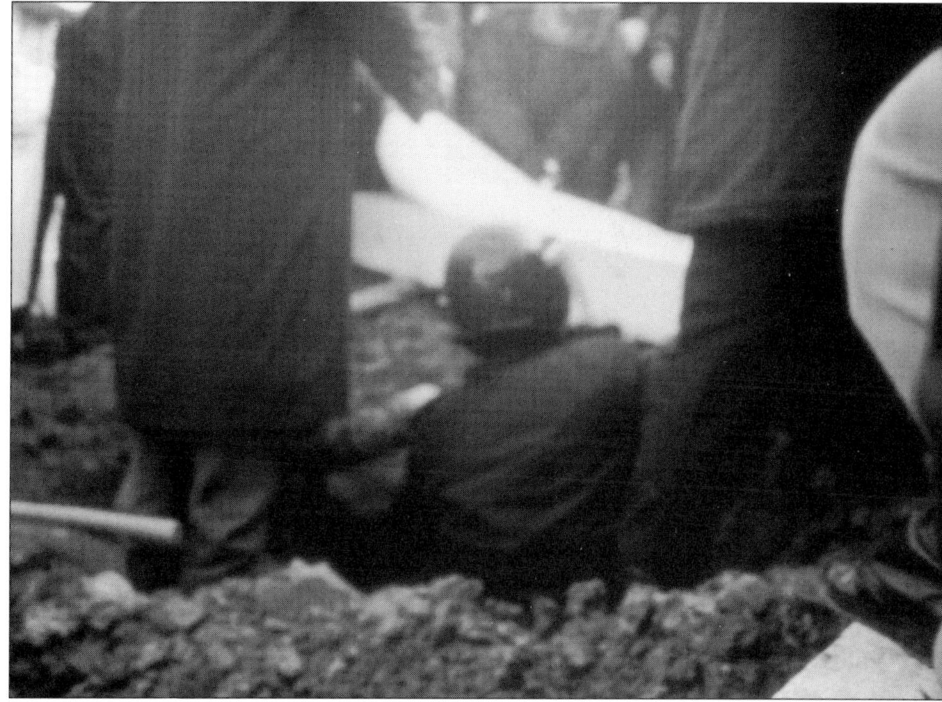

Police bury the bodies of prisoners who died of head injuries after police and gendarmes entered Ümraniye Special Type Prison to quell a protest. Police or gendarmes brought into prisons often use such opportunities to "punish" remand or convicted political prisoners by inflicting savage beatings.
© Ş. Dayanan

been no progress in human rights protection in Turkey, but instead a serious deterioration?

The state within the state — a barrier to change

The critical and unresolved issue is the extent of civil authority over the security apparatus. The security forces, comprising the police and gendarmerie as well as the military and the intelligence agencies, continue to have great influence and power in Turkey, effectively functioning as a state within a state. Although it is 12 years since the formal end of military rule, elected politicians are constantly reminded of their junior status.

While he was in opposition Mesut Yılmaz, who became Prime Minister in March 1996, openly addressed the problem of the balance of state power, while investigating abuses by soldiers in Tunceli province. He referred to a fact-finding mission by former Deputy Prime Minister Murat Karayalçın in October 1994, which the military authorities prevented from visiting settlements allegedly burned by the security forces, and said:

> *"In a country in which even the Deputy Prime Minister cannot go to evacuated villages, I leave it to you to imagine what kind of influence the opposition parties can exert. In order for an opposition party to do its job properly, civil authority must first be sovereign. At the moment civil authority is not in charge in Tunceli. The chain of command does not operate according to the principle of the superiority of civilian authority ... After Mrs Ciller came to power, the fight against terror was handed over wholesale to military units."*[38]

Whereas a Turkish government could gain credit at home and abroad by upholding its citizens' human rights, increased supervision of the security apparatus and a determined drive to punish those responsible for human rights violations would erode the power of the state within the state and as such is strongly opposed by the security forces. In the face of such opposition the government will require considerable courage and commitment to press through an agenda of reform.

The security forces are the most important link in the chain. The basic safeguards contained in the Turkish Constitution and Criminal Procedure Code, as well as the European Convention on Human Rights, the UN Convention against Torture and other international standards that form part of Turkish law, count for nothing unless they are applied by the police officers and gendarmes in the streets, police stations and rural areas. But the security forces strongly resist change, human rights reform and, in particular, civilian supervision for two main reasons.

Firstly there is a widely held suspicion that no concession will be sufficient to satisfy those at home and abroad who criticize Turkey's human rights record, because their true aim is partition of the country. Yet there seems little basis for this concern. The fact is that Amnesty International and other international non-governmental organizations neither advocate nor even talk of partition. Those foreign governments who have raised the issue of human rights most strongly in recent years are Turkey's long-standing allies and are presumably committed to the integrity of its borders.

Secondly, and more importantly, any determined move for reform which increased civilian supervision of security methods would result in increased power for civilian government and consequent reduction of the security forces' influence in Turkish society. Expenditure on the security apparatus accounts for a significant proportion of the annual budget and it enjoys a host of economic and political privileges. Less power for the security forces could put those privileges at risk. Tens of thousands of civil servants have aligned themselves with the supremacy of the security forces and depend on this for their position in the administration, their housing, jobs and other privileges. They clearly have an interest in maintaining the politically dominant role of the security state.

International experience demonstrates that where there is no civilian supervision of the security forces' activities, standards decline and dubious practices begin to proliferate. The result is a progression into disorder and widespread abuse. In the case of the Turkish security forces, the impunity with which they commit human rights violations and their immunity from normal checks and controls has resulted in a drift into criminal abuses. This can be seen in the increasing use of proxy forces in the military campaign against the PKK and other armed opposition groups.

Violations by proxy

The use of proxies was an important factor — perhaps the key factor — in the dramatic increase of "disappearances" and extrajudicial executions in the early 1990s. One group of proxies are "confessors", convicted members of the armed opposition unofficially recruited by the security forces to attack their former comrades. "Confessors" have been implicated in several extrajudicial executions. The 1995 report of the Parliamentary Commission on Unsolved Political Killings expresses barely suppressed outrage that the Turkish security forces should harbour "confessors" and condone their illegal activities:

> *"Confessors, sheltering under the protection of the state, and even being housed in residential quarters purchased for state police in Diyarbakır city, take advantage of the state's failure to exercise proper influence over them in order to establish crime networks involved in such offences as arms smuggling, murder and drugs smuggling. It has been established by this commission that several cases in which confessors were apprehended in connection with such offences were covered up on the intervention of high-ranking public servants."*

It is also a matter of record that "confessors" have been brought from prison to participate in security force operations. One such "confessor" addressed a court with a plea for remission on the grounds that he had hunted several "heads" for the state.

Such irregular practices convey an extraordinary picture of a slack and lawless security establishment engaging in criminal acts.

Evidence given in court by village guards involved in the abduction and murder of Şerif Avşar confirms that Turkish security forces deliberately plan extrajudicial executions by proxy. Village guards who detained Şerif Avşar in Diyarbakır in April 1994 told Diyarbakır Criminal Court that his killing had been carefully planned, on orders given by a named gendarme commander. According to one guard, after interrogation Şerif Avşar was taken "to a shabby building located 19 kilometres outside the city. [X] called me in and told me to shoot Avşar and I obeyed orders." Another village guard admitted that they had carried out similar operations in the past on the orders of various commanders: "If we had not obeyed orders we would have been sacked."

While there may be valid reasons to arm village guards for the protection of their own settlements, the routine use of untrained village guards as an auxiliary force accompanying gendarmes on security raids on neighbouring villages and even on cross-border operations into northern Iraq, contributes to conditions in which human rights violations are more likely to occur. The authority and responsibilities of village guards while carrying out searches, for example, are not laid down, as they are for police officers, in a formal code of conduct. Village guards do not undergo a full program of training, and are not part of a clear chain-of-command structure.

On the one hand, village guards complain that they are exploited: made to face the PKK without adequate weaponry or support or made to sweep dangerous territory ahead of regular forces. On the other hand, in the rural areas of the southeast, where tribal relations are still important, there are many reports that village guard chiefs exploit their status to exercise local tyranny and settle private scores. The village guard system was severely criticized by the Commission on Unsolved Political

Village guards in southeast Turkey. © Hollandse Hoogte

Killings, which described it as an investment in social discord.

Turkey, which has one of the world's largest standing armies, presumably resorts to such measures, not for lack of manpower, but because armed irregulars outside the chain of command are a convenient tool. Similar paramilitary forces in other countries are often used by the state to commit human rights violations while denying official responsibility. The system as it stands leaves the villager isolated and exposed while the PKK and the state compete to terrorize the community in the belief that whoever exerts the greatest fear will get the support of the people.

These developments are not just a threat for Kurdish farmers in Siirt and Şırnak. The abuses and routine brutality learned in the southeast are being exported to the rest of Turkey. A simple example is the practice of unsupervised detention.

Security raids on villages in southeast Turkey are carried out with little or no judicial supervision, leaving protection of the human rights of villagers to the conscience of the individual soldier. In such operations in remote areas, record-keeping becomes a vital safeguard against "disappearances". Dozens of villagers "disappeared" in villages around Diyarbakır in late 1993 and 1994, and failure to record their initial detention was a key factor. When villagers applied to courts and local governors for information about the fate of relatives seen marched away by soldiers, the officials and the government could only express ignorance. It appears that no records were kept of such operations. What were technically police operations were carried out more like military attacks. There was apparently no supervision by judges or prosecutors. The presence of a prosecutor or judge during operations in villages and scrupulous record-keeping are not necessarily cast-iron safeguards, but the absence of such precautions is practically an invitation to the security forces to commit abuses.

Police in Istanbul and Ankara had long been using torture in interrogating detainees, but it was not until well into the 1990s that they began to routinely deny holding detainees or to register

---

Right: ***A villager from the southeast joins the families of the "disappeared" in a sit-down protest in Istanbul. Many villagers "disappeared" in late 1993 and 1994 in village raids but no records were kept of these security operations. The absence of any safeguards for the civilian population in such operations is an invitation to the security forces to commit human rights abuses. © Ş. Dayanan***

them several days late — behaviour quite obviously learned by officers on tours of duty in the southeast. This in turn led to the first reports of "disappearance" in the big cities of the west.

Turkish citizens should not believe that the disrespect for basic human rights standards presents a risk "only in the southeast", or "only for terrorists". The gendarmerie officer allegedly responsible for torturing six youths, one of them 15 years old, at Mordoğan Gendarmerie Post in Izmir in December 1994, was newly returned from duties in the Van province of the region under emergency legislation. The youths, accused of theft, were subjected to severe beatings, *falaka*, and electric shocks. Three claimed that they had been handcuffed to a radio mast in the gendarmerie yard and left exposed to rain and cold weather for three days. A television company actually filmed one of the detainees cuffed to the mast. After six days' detention the detainees were taken for a medical examination at Mordoğan Health Centre where, apparently under pressure from the gendarmerie post, the doctor recorded no signs of ill-treatment. However, a second examination at the Karaburun Forensic Medicine Centre revealed extensive bruising, burns and marks of trauma.

Safeguards will not be effective unless they are upheld throughout the ranks of the security forces, supervised by internal inspectors and commissions, prosecutors, and parliament. Breaches of proper practice must be investigated by judicial bodies offering guarantees of independence and impartiality and leading to the bringing to justice of those responsible.

Impunity: the major obstacle

A security force which is ridden with flawed and improper practices, in which individual soldiers have the power to kill with impunity is both inefficient and dangerous. Supervision and control of the army, gendarmerie and police force should be a primary task of government. However, the previous coalition governments under Prime Ministers Süleyman Demirel and Tansu Çiller seem to have abdicated this responsibility, preferring to give the security chiefs a free reign. The government formed in March 1996 was no more determined to take a strong hand. The five highest ranking police, military and state officials who presided over the security forces' descent into a mire of questionable and illegal practices were elected into parliament in December 1995 and two became cabinet ministers.

Faced with an intense internal conflict and situated in a region of considerable political instability, the government will need to find courage and determination if it is to rein in the abuses of its security forces. The impunity which has protected police and gendarmerie from punishment for human rights violations during more than a decade of conflict in the southeast has been extended to police and gendarmes for abuses committed in Istanbul and Ankara.

Discipline and supervision by the civilian government and the judiciary would mean thoroughly investigating military and police abuses, and punishing the perpetrators with the full force of the law at a time when police officers are being gunned down in the streets of the capital and young men are being killed every day in the mountains by members of armed opposition groups. Nevertheless, the promise of decisive action to safeguard fundamental freedoms retains considerable appeal for the Turkish public.

Decisive action it must be, however, and the time is long overdue. Vague and private exhortations for the police to behave better will not be sufficient. After the ECPT announced in 1993 that they had found a piece of torture equipment in Ankara Police Headquarters, there were no reports of disciplinary measures or prosecutions. Two years later, in February 1995, Prime Minister Tansu Çiller sent a confidential circular to the Interior Minister demanding that "Whatever the alleged crime, suspects shall not be subjected to ill-treatment ... police stations shall be inspected and tools capable of being used in ill-treatment shall be removed." In April 1995 Şahabettin Özaslaner was detained and interrogated by officers of the Anti-Terror Branch of Ankara Police Headquarters. He later told Amnesty International that he had been tortured while strapped to a device his interrogators called the "torture table", the same apparatus found by the ECPT.

7

Amnesty International's recommendations

Amnesty International's recommendations to the Turkish Government are few and simple. They will not be expensive to implement. They are not a counsel of perfection, but the minimum that must be done to stop the main human rights violations.

The recommended changes will offer suspected members of armed organizations no more protection than that which every Turkish citizen deserves by right against torture, extrajudicial execution and "disappearance", but which successive governments have so far refused to grant. These recommendations are not a "compromise with terrorism" and are not designed to undermine the effectiveness or the legitimate powers of the security forces. For the most part, they are simply a restatement of principles already recognized in Turkish law and in the Turkish Constitution.

The recommendations also reflect international human rights law and standards such as the European Convention on Human Rights, the UN Convention against Torture, and other instruments. It is important to emphasize that these instruments are not foreign charters, inappropriate to the Turkish situation, but instruments which were shaped with the participation and approval of Turkish governments, and those which are in the form of treaties were freely ratified by the Turkish parliament. More importantly, under the terms of Article 90 of the Turkish Constitution, they form an integral part of Turkish domestic law.

These recommendations will not endanger public security, nor the security of police officers. They will, however, help to ensure the personal security of Turkish citizens for whom there can be no true security until their human rights are respected and protected. In short, these recommendations are no more than an appeal for the Turkish Government and parliament to require its own state servants to observe the rule of law. It is difficult to imagine or propose a more modest objective.

Recommendations to the Government of Turkey

1. The Turkish Government should implement the recommendations contained in the November 1993 report of the UN Committee against Torture — specifically: that all detainees, including those detained on suspicion of offences under the Anti-Terror Law, should be given access to legal counsel, and that the maximum period of police detention should be reduced from the present maximum of 30 days so that detainees are brought before a judge without delay. Incommunicado detention should be abolished.

2. The government should accede to the ICCPR.

3. The government should establish proper registration procedures for detainees, which are consistent with international standards, and sanctions to ensure that they are scrupulously observed.

4. The government should publicly express concern about the increase in allegations of extrajudicial execution and "disappearance", and extend invitations to the UN Special Rapporteur on extrajudicial, summary or arbitrary executions, as well as the Working Group on Enforced or Involuntary Disappearances, to visit the country in 1997.

5. The government should conduct thorough, prompt and impartial investigations into the cases of the scores of people who have reportedly "disappeared" in security force custody since 1991, as required by the UN Declaration on the Protection of All Persons from Enforced Disappearance.

6. The government should ensure that village guards are not used as paramilitaries in operations, identity checks and roadblocks beyond the immediate vicinity of their village. There should be clear chain-of-command responsibility over the village guards and those responsible for human rights violations should be held to account.

7. All reports of extrajudicial execution should be fully investigated in accordance with the UN Principles on the Effective Prevention and Investigation of Extra-legal, Arbitrary and Summary Executions.

8. All prisoners of conscience should be immediately and unconditionally released; Article 8 of the Anti-Terror Law, which provides for up to three years' imprisonment for allegedly "separatist" statements, even where no advocacy of violence has been made, should be reformed or repealed along with other relevant articles of the penal code under which prisoners of conscience are being held. Judges should be clearly instructed that imprisonment for expression of non-violent opinions violates international treaties signed by Turkey.

9. The Turkish authorities should ensure that the Law on the Prosecution of Civil Servants (which permits local governors to block prosecutions of security forces personnel) is not applied to allegations of extrajudicial execution, "disappearance", torture or ill-treatment by police or other civil servants.

10. All remand and convicted prisoners should be guarded by officers under the authority of the Ministry of Justice as soon as they are detained, and never by police or gendarmerie officers.

11. The government should abolish the death penalty.

12. The government should scrupulously observe the internationally recognized principle of non-*refoulement* and accordingly should not forcibly return any person to a country where he or she would be at risk of human rights violations. To ensure effective protection for non-European refugee and asylum-seekers, the Turkish Government should remove the geographic limitation which it maintains to the 1951 Convention relating to the Status of Refugees and ensure the necessary legal measures are taken to formally recognize their rights under Turkish law.

13. The government should ensure that all law-enforcement personnel and members of the security forces receive effective training on national and international standards which protect human rights and humanitarian law and how to enforce them properly.

Recommendations to the international community

To UN member states:

1. Urge the Government of Turkey to invite the UN Working Group on Enforced or Involuntary Disappearances, the UN Special Rapporteur on torture, and the UN Special Rapporteur on extrajudicial, summary or arbitrary executions to visit.

2. Urge the Government of Turkey to enact the safeguards recommended by the UN Committee against Torture in its report of November 1993.

3. Encourage the Government of Turkey to ensure that Turkey accedes to the ICCPR and to its two Optional Protocols and to make a declaration under Article 41 recognizing the competence of the Human Rights Committee to receive communications by states.

4. Urge the Government of Turkey to act promptly on the recommendations made on individual cases raised by the Working Group on Arbitrary Detention

5. Encourage Turkey to lift its geographical limitation to the 1951 Convention relating to the Status of Refugees and its 1967 Protocol.

6. To make sure that arms are not used to commit human rights abuses, ensure that governments which supply military equipment and training to the Turkish armed forces obtain guarantees, supported by end-use monitoring, that the arms are not used to commit or facilitate human rights violations.

To the Committee of Ministers of the Council of Europe:

1. Urge the Government of Turkey to enact the safeguards recommended by the European Committee for the Prevention of Torture.

2. Urge the Government of Turkey to establish impartial and expert investigations into the continuing allegations of extrajudicial execution and "disappearance".

To OSCE member states:

Urge the Government of Turkey to invite a fact-finding mission to investigate suppression of freedom of expression, harassment of human rights defenders, and violations of the right to life.

To EU member states:

Sustain close monitoring of freedom of expression in Turkey, as recommended by the European Parliament in its approval of the 1995 Customs Union, and use all means at their disposal to encourage the Government of Turkey to effect genuine reform of those laws under which prisoners of conscience are held.

Recommendations to armed opposition groups

1. Armed opposition groups should publicly undertake to observe common Article 3 of the Geneva Conventions and other humanitarian laws applicable to internal conflicts.

2. Armed opposition group leaders should inform their members of their responsibilities under common Article 3 and take effective steps to prevent breaches of humanitarian law. They should issue clear orders to their forces prohibiting deliberate and arbitrary killings and torture of prisoners (including captured village guards) and those not taking a direct part in the conflict under all circumstances, as well as indiscriminate attacks on the civilian population.

3. Under no circumstances should alleged informers or collaborators be ill-treated, tortured or executed.

Endnotes

1 *Reuters*, 1 July 1995

2 The Turkish Armed Forces seized power in 1960, 1971 and 1980. On 27 May 1960 the military put an end to the rule of the Democratic Party under Prime Minister Adnan Menderes. He and two ministers were executed. The military take-over of 12 March 1971 was directed against the Turkish parliament and aimed at destroying a radical movement of intellectuals, students and trade unionists. After political violence in the late 1970s had claimed 5,000 lives, the military staged a further coup in 1980, establishing martial law throughout the country and suspending all political activity until 1983. In that year a general election resulted in a return to civilian rule under the Motherland Party, with Turgut Özal as Prime Minister. General Kenan Evren, leader of the military coup, remained President until 1990.

3 *Cumhuriyet* (Republic), 28 October 1994

4 *Separatist Terror in the Özal Period (1983-1991)*, Tekin Yayinevi, 1992, p121

5 *Reuters*, 9 June 1995

6 *Cumhuriyet*, 4 September 1994

7 Shoes have become a symbol in relatives' campaign for the "disappeared". The shoes which Metin Can, President of Elaziğ Human Rights Association, had been wearing when he was abducted on 21 February 1993 were found some days later placed near his home. When he was found dead, there were no shoes on his body, which showed signs of torture.

8 In its 1992 public statement the ECPT emphasized that it had received allegation of torture, corroborated by medical evidence, from people detained in connection with common criminal offences.

9 Article 19 of Law 2253

10 UN document E/CN.4/1995/36, para 402

11 *Z. Aksoy v. Turkey*, 21987/93

12 Quoted in *Ataturk's Children — Turkey and the Kurds*, Jonathan Rugman, Cassell 1996

13 The exact number of evacuated or burned villages is almost impossible to establish, since some villages are comprised of several settlements, each with its own name, spread over many square miles. Some districts of a village might be burned while others are spared. Some burned villages have later been reoccupied. In October 1994 the HRA stated that 1,334 villages had been evacuated or

destroyed. In May 1996 the Emergency Region Governor reported that 2,297 settlements had been evacuated.

14 Article 31 report considering the case of Zeki Aksoy who was shot and killed by unidentified assailants in April 1994 (see Chapter 3).

15 Turkish Criminal Procedure Code, Article 128

16 The failure to do so is contrary to international standards requiring registers in all places of detention, namely Articles 2 and 3 of the UN Declaration on the Protection of All Persons from Enforced Disappearance, Rule 7 of the Standard Minimum Rules for the Treatment of Prisoners and Principle 12 of the UN Body of Principles for the Protection of All Persons under Any Form of Detention or Imprisonment.

17 Report of the Working Group on Enforced or Involuntary Disappearances, Paragraph 399, (E/CN.4/1995/36)

18 Turkish Medical Association, *The Report on the Health Services and Health Personnel's Problems in the Southeast*; Ankara March 1995, p42

19 For more information about the role of medical professionals in the campaign to protect human rights worldwide, see: *Prescription for change: health professionals and the exposure of human rights violations*, AI Index: ACT 75/01/96

20 Article 12 of the UN Convention against Torture

21 In May 1996 the Turkish Embassy in London released figures on convictions of police officers for ill-treatment and torture. There were 15 convictions in 1994, and 20 in 1995. The lightest sentences were one-and-a-half months' imprisonment, the heaviest three years. It was not indicated whether these sentences were suspended, quashed or upheld on appeal.

22 unrelated to the Lebanese group of the same name

23 *Reuters*, 18 September 1995

24 Statement by the Turkish Ambassador to the UN in Geneva, 24 November 1993

25 Report of the UN Special Rapporteur on extrajudicial, summary or arbitrary executions (December 1994, E/CN.4/1995/61)

26 Report of the UN Special Rapporteur on torture (January 1995, E/CN.4/1995/34)

27 An invitation was extended to the Special Rapporteur on the promotion and protection of the right of freedom of opinion and expression to visit in 1995, but a firm date was never given and the visit had not taken place by mid-1996.

[28] *Turkish Daily News*, 2 August 1994

[29] *Cumhuriyet*, 16 February 1996

[30] Public statement received by Egyptian members of Amnesty International in January 1996

[31] In 1993 the Chief of General Staff General Doğan Güreş referred to events in the southeast as "low intensity conflict".

[32] *Cumhuriyet*, 10 May 1995

[33] In May 1996 Amnesty International received a government reply stating that "Ali Karaca, from the village of Güleç, was detained by local security forces on 6 October 1994. However, because of his poor state of health, Mr Karaca was released and sent to the nearest hospital. His family was informed accordingly. He died some days later in the hospital of Elazığ due to his illness".

[34] UN Register on Conventional Arms for 1993 and 1994.

[35] Paragraph 4, (b), [I] of the *Principles Governing Conventional Arms Transfers*.

[36] *Cumhuriyet*, 28 November 1993

[37] Proceedings of a Council of Europe Colloquium: *Le médecin et les droits de l'homme*, March 1982. Strasbourg: Council of Europe, 1985, p.155

[38] *Cumhuriyet*, 4 August 1995.